Praise for *I*

'As our lives move online, we're all carried along by a vast ocean of data ... Well informed, well researched and very readable, *Disconnect* by Jordan Guiao helps us navigate the great data ocean. It helps us identify these big phenomena and how they affect us as individuals. Armed with that understanding, we're better equipped to survive the data ocean's most terrifying tempests.'
– Ed Santow, Australia's former human rights commissioner and professor of responsible technology at the University of Technology Sydney

'A necessary reset of a book ... Given how many of us are losing loved ones to conspiracy rabbit holes and brain-shaping tech, this humane, insightful and – yes – practical book couldn't be more timely.'
– Benjamin Law, writer, broadcaster and author of *The Family Law*

'Jordan Guiao is a digital native who brings our disordered online world into focus through the characters in a terrifying new story – many of whom we will have already met in our own social media feed. Guiao fuses personal stories with professional insight, and the result is refreshingly empathetic and practical. *Disconnect* is both a cautionary tale and a sorely needed rallying call to reclaim a healthy internet.'
– Ed Coper, author of *Facts and Other Lies* and executive director of the Center for Impact Communications

'What do we do when our friends fall prey to conspiracy theories, dating scams or online abuse? When our children become depressed because they can't live up to a social media ideal? Jordan Guiao's *Disconnect* dissects how social media platforms have been used to exploit our vulnerabilities and what happens to the people who are targeted online. Thankfully, this timely book doesn't reduce such problems to moral panics. Instead, Guiao builds complex case studies of freedom fighters and anti-vaxxers, screen addicts, abusers and victims, offering useful insights into the power of social media to alter our worldviews and polarise societies. His case that it's time to act to rein in this power comes with practical suggestions about how to change our relationships with technology.'

– Fiona R. Martin, associate professor in online and convergent media at The University of Sydney

Disconnect

Disconnect

Why we get pushed to extremes online and how to stop it

Jordan Guiao

MONASH
UNIVERSITY
PUBLISHING

Published by Monash University Publishing
Matheson Library Annexe
40 Exhibition Walk
Monash University
Clayton, Victoria 3800, Australia
publishing.monash.edu/

Monash University Publishing: the discussion starts here

9781922633354 (paperback)
9781922633361 (pdf)
9781922633378 (epub)

A catalogue record for this
book is available from the
National Library of Australia

Cover design by Daniel Benneworth-Gray
Typesetting by Typography Studio
Cover photography by Will Salkeld

Published with kind support from The Australia Institute's Centre
for Responsible Technology

Printed in Australia by Griffin Press

For Tim,
who makes me want to build a better world

Contents

Introduction

Sometime around 2019, my friend became a conspiracy theorist. It was subtle at first: a strange YouTube video post here, a rant I couldn't quite understand there. I originally dismissed this as him being a contrarian who enjoyed arguments too much. Then it got serious. In group chats, he would respond to topics such as elections or public health with shocking fervour. His once entertaining banter deteriorated into essay-length sermons. He would get angry at the rest of the group for not seeing his point of view, even as those viewpoints became increasingly esoteric and incomprehensible. He would rail on about some secret cabal of 'elites' and a great, shadowy 'They' who were conspiring against everyday people and making up global hoaxes. He would insist we watch less-than-credible YouTube videos that 'proved' his claims and link to propaganda websites that allegedly did the same.

It was unexpected, and at first my friends and I tried to overlook it. Some of us had longstanding friendships with him. Then it settled into a pattern of awkwardness. Eventually, our group of friends learned to avoid potentially triggering topics around him. Contributing to the group chat became like tiptoeing through a field of buried grenades, any one ready to explode with just a foot placed wrong. Yet even as we trained ourselves to keep conversations light and airy, he would find ways to draw things back to his favourite topics of ire. Message chains would inevitably descend into tirades, with him shouting wildly at all of us and no one responding.

I'd read about this type of behaviour, but this was the first person I knew who had a shift in personality due to things he read online. He would not be the last.

During the Covid-19 pandemic, some members of my family became vaccine-hesitant. Despite believing in the science of vaccinations before the pandemic, even insisting on them for their children, the fear, uncertainty and concern over the novel coronavirus, coupled with a normalisation of anti-science rhetoric online and a barrage of disinformation from the social media personalities they followed, had made them question whether they would get vaccinated until it was forced upon them.

I feel uncomfortable and a little guilty as I write about this, because I value those relationships and do not want to damage them. But these are the facts.

Sometimes, relationships can be ruined by behavioural changes caused by online interaction. A person I once considered one of my best friends became such a social media narcissist that it damaged our relationship, and over time we fell out. Her vibrancy devolved into one-dimensional shallowness. I watched as she discarded genuine friendship after genuine friendship for those that would benefit her online persona and bolster the character she was creating for herself on social media. I mourned her transformation from an authentic, messy, beautiful person into a deeply insecure actress, turning her life into a highly stylised production in the hopes of online fame. We haven't spoken in years.

Introduction

Something is happening that is turning smart, rational individuals into pathological caricatures, and it's to do with being online.

I pay attention to these issues because I work as a researcher for the Australia Institute's Centre for Responsible Technology. Over the last few years, I have noticed that people around me have begun to voice the same observations – a friend from uni, a distant uncle, a colleague from that job eight years ago, a next-door neighbour, the parent of their child's friend is turning into a social media narcissist, an online conspiracy theorist, an anti-vaxxer 'freedom fighter', a troll. Sometimes this hits closer to home: a son or daughter has become a gaming addict, a mother is a dating app maniac, a cousin has become enmeshed in internet forums of dubious origin. Like a highly transmissible strain of Covid-19, this phenomenon has spread outward and proliferated, until it seems we all know someone who has fallen down one of these rabbit holes.

We are, without a doubt, living in strange times. The pandemic has coerced even the most reluctant among us into a digital world. It has created a new breed of remote workers, forced many to swap physical interactions for the artificial intimacy of Zoom, and encouraged us to shop, play and study in front of our computers. We live more of our lives online now than we have at any previous point in history, and humanity has reached this significant milestone very quickly. We can be certain that this speed has impacted us in ways we are only beginning to understand.

When I began thinking about this book, I wanted to test out the theory that we all knew one of these types. I talked openly to different groups of people as I shared the book's premise. I was validated by the knowing reactions, cautious nods and offers of names to talk to. 'My father is like that …', 'My sister is …', 'You should talk to …'. Compelled and encouraged, I sought to speak to people navigating these online challenges, looking to understand their stories. In the process I had to examine my own behaviours with the internet and what had led me down this line of inquiry in the first place.

Let me start with a confession, or perhaps a disclaimer: I am, without question, an internet addict. I clock up an average of seven hours a day of screen time.

My internet addiction started early. In 1996, when Dad first connected our Apple Macintosh Performa 5400CD to our telephone line using a screeching modem, I was hooked immediately. I discovered chatrooms with people around the world. I found solace with other like-minded sci-fi nerds who posted about movies and fictional characters. As a teenager, I guiltily discovered parts of the internet I probably shouldn't have been exploring, and that my parents and siblings did not know how to access. I even dabbled with being a bit of a troll. I regret trolling now, of course – but back then I simply didn't understand the impact it could have.

I built a career out of the internet. In the early 2000s, after failing to secure a gig as a Disney animator, I turned instead to digital media, and found a solid career path in digital production and communications. I scrubbed my online persona clean and began anew. To me, the internet was nothing short of magic. What enamoured me was not the nuts and bolts of the technology, but how people used it to connect and communicate. You could find tribes who shared your niche interests. Distance and geography became irrelevant as you talked to people on the other side of the globe. If a confessional bent took you, you could publish your thoughts and have them read by thousands almost instantly. Back then, the internet's potential as a communication tool was inspiring. Back then, the internet felt full of promise and possibility.

As I honed my expertise on the internet and its impact on communications and culture, that optimism sustained itself – for me, if not for society at large. There was a marked shift in the public conversation during the 2010s, as more people realised the darker and less-than-healthy applications of the internet. But I never questioned my own obsession with the web until I reached what I thought was the pinnacle of my career – a job in Silicon Valley. After almost fifteen years as a digital strategist, working with some of Australia's largest and most dynamic media companies and many of the Big Tech companies, such as Facebook, Google, Twitter and Apple, I needed to see if I could make it at the mecca for digital and technology professionals. In 2018, I moved to California.

At first, I only saw the highlights of this silicon wonderland. The perks of being a regular client of social networks were extensive: free lunches at Big Tech campuses, rooftop meetings with fresh organic juices, yoga sessions after workshops, inventive merchandise. Yet, as I lived in the San Francisco Bay Area, I gradually began to see a different side. The Bay Area suffers from a severe problem of human displacement. Entire groups have been forced to relocate or face homelessness as the tech boom has prompted skyrocketing real estate prices and spiralling costs of living. Most property buyers are tech workers.[1] Newly minted millionaires are common as tech companies go from startup to IPO. With each batch of tech companies going public, the housing crisis deepens, as wealthy tech workers continue to push up prices. In 2019, *Vox* ran an article on how even programmers with six-figure salaries are struggling to afford studio apartments in the area.[2] The situation in San Francisco is so bad that the United

Nations has deemed the housing shortage and resulting homelessness a 'human rights violation'.[3] It was hard to ignore the homeless people wandering around San Francisco when I literally had to sidestep their faeces on sidewalks.

My cousin, an intensive-care nurse at what used to be called San Francisco General Hospital but is now Zuckerberg General Hospital (after the Zuckerbergs gifted the hospital its largest-ever single donation in 2015), saw the human cost of displacement firsthand. 'We have more and more homeless and sick people who are simply no longer in control of their lives,' he told me. The Bay Area felt like it was divided into two classes: those who worked in the tech industry and those who did not. It was hard not to correlate the social cost of technological progress with the human displacement. Big Tech companies can't take all the blame for global inequality, but they have amplified it, and ushered in many other issues besides.

It was this experience that led me to question my utopian vision of the internet and made me look harder at how it affects society in developed countries the world over. If the internet was meant to be one of the best communication tools we had to offer, why was it making people confused? Why was it leaving the most vulnerable among us prone to scammers and fraudsters? Why was it making us angrier than ever? Why was it causing rational people to seem crazy? While it was keeping families in touch and sparking new friendships, at a more fundamental level, was it beginning to divide society?

Recently, we have begun to see the effects of internet-related issues. Research draws the linkages between social media platforms and body disorders, trolling and mental health issues, coordinated online campaigns and violent protests. Facebook's brand has become so deleterious, as evidence of the platform's continued harm and negligence

6

continues to build, that many believe the company's rebranding as Meta was a way to distance themselves from the bad publicity. Their own research, leaked by whistleblower Frances Haugen, showed that Instagram (which is owned by Meta) was toxic for young people, especially teenage girls, who experienced increased issues around body image, anxiety and depression. Teenage boys aren't immune, with the *The Wall Street Journal* recounting, 'In their report on body image in 2020, Facebook's researchers found that 40% of teen boys experience negative social comparison.' It quoted one participant in the research: '"I just feel on the edge a lot of the time," a teen boy in the U.S. told Facebook's researchers. "It's like you can be called out for anything you do. One wrong move. One wrong step."'[4] This is confirmed by external research showing that social media is causing an epidemic of mental health problems among young people, and that Instagram is particularly bad for their mental wellbeing.[5]

Facebook also knew about the harmful conspiracy theories that circulated in the lead-up to the 2020 US election, culminating in the shocking and violent riots at the US Capitol. The company did little to intervene. On 6 January 2021, user reports of 'false news' hit nearly 40,000 per hour and threats of violence were rife, as staff expressed alarm on Facebook's internal Workplace site. As *The Washington Post* noted, 'The company's internal research over several years had identified ways to diminish the spread of political polarization, conspiracy theories and incitements to violence but … in many instances, executives had declined to implement those steps.'[6]

Facebook was aware of hate speech and calls for violence against minority ethnic groups in India and Myanmar but did little about it.[7] For years, its algorithms promoted posts that provoked angry reactions over neutral or positive ones. There's evidence of the platform being used for human trafficking and illegal activities such as recruiting hitmen.[8] This litany of issues are only some recent instances to have made the headlines, and many continue unresolved.

Google's YouTube has been similarly plagued, with issues around mis- and disinformation, including around the pandemic and political campaigns, going unchecked. Misinformation is shared without malicious intent, while disinformation is deliberately false and shared as part of a campaign of persuasion. YouTube's algorithm recommends videos that violate the company's own content policies, promoting content that includes violence, hate speech and scams.[9] YouTube has been consistently cited as a platform where users can be radicalised – including the infamous 2019 Christchurch mosque shooter, who a New Zealand royal commission found had used Facebook and YouTube as a source of inspiration and promotion.[10] YouTube's response is too often to make minor tweaks or changes to community standards that do little to truly address the quagmire, as misogynistic, violent and disturbing content continues to be shared.

Chinese company ByteDance owns TikTok, whose algorithms have been revealed to have biases against people of colour, while its company's moderators to have encouraged users to remove videos of those with disabilities and those it deems unattractive, as part of efforts to 'curate an aspirational air in the videos it promotes'.[11] Its AI clumsily recommends harmful content, including about eating disorders and mental health issues. A joint investigation by the ABC's *Four Corners* and Triple J's *Hack* included the case of Lauren Hemmings, who developed an eating disorder four months after joining TikTok and being bombarded with images of fitness influencers and videos on calorie counting: 'I was no longer seeing funny dance videos or anything. It was just like this complete focus on that fitness and healthy lifestyle goal … I felt that I could not eat anything without knowing how many calories it contained and without meeting my target number of calories throughout the day … Before TikTok, calorie counting had never crossed my path.'[12]

It is on these platforms that many of us connect and communicate, do business and seek out entertainment. Some describe Big Tech as 'the new Big Tobacco' – with smoking once widely encouraged, only years later did governments realise its harmful effects on health and the role of tobacco companies in fostering addiction, and begin to legislate around such companies' practices. Many issues about public health and safety are unresolved when it comes to the world's largest social networks and online companies, who continue to rake in massive profits and march on with their relentless growth and increasing reach.

Various critics are taking the fight directly to these platforms, including governments, regulators, academics and civil society. There are attempts to curb Big Tech's influence through antitrust law, data privacy regulation, online safety initiatives and significant lawsuits. I feel privileged to be part of one of those institutions taking the fight directly to Big Tech. The Australia Institute's Centre for Responsible Technology fights battles at the institutional level, seeking to hold Big Tech companies to account, influence governments on technology policy and partner with academics, industry and civil society to focus the public's attention on the most important online issues we are facing today. These efforts are vitally important: the tech companies must be held to account at a system-wide level, given their enormous influence and the resources they invest in lobbying to minimise regulation and changes that may harm their business models.

But I wanted to write this book because what I felt was lacking was a way to relate these enormous and urgent issues to the everyday person.

The statistics in academic studies, media articles and industry research – it all represents individuals and their stories. There is little emphasis in the reports and research on problematic internet use about the people who are navigating these issues. They are members of our community: mothers, fathers, grandparents, sons, daughters, sisters, brothers, cousins, uncles, aunts, friends, colleagues, parent-group buddies, acquaintances, neighbours, exes. If most of us know, or know of, someone who has got into trouble online, how can we understand how they reached this point? How can we talk to them without isolating them? How can we point them towards recognising and changing their behaviours? Rather than describing online issues in the conceptual and abstract, I wanted to add the intimacy of personal stories and individual experiences.

There may be confronting truths some of us need to face – some relationships can't survive when one party has been radicalised by the internet. Some people may simply be too far down the rabbit hole. They may not recognise that they have a problem, or be willing to be part of any intervention, or want to be rehabilitated. There are also those who are unrepentant extremists: who actively exploit others by spreading hate and disinformation on the internet. This book is not an apology or a plea for understanding for such people, who should be held to account for their actions, legally and morally. Violence, threats and the spreading of hatred and mayhem should never be condoned or excused.

But for every such extremist, there are many more everyday internet users whose engagement with the internet has become problematic, and the story of why is complex and deserving of discussion. As a researcher, I've come across examples in the literature of those who have entered a bleak place only to find a perspective that has helped them re-emerge saner and wiser, so there is always hope. And if even one relationship is mended through this book, the effort of writing it has been worthwhile.

Each chapter is themed around a persona – a freedom fighter, an online gamer and so on – and seeks to unpack the psychology of the condition, as well as the broader context and environment, aiming to shed light on potential paths through addiction. I share stories and case studies of those who have shown problematic behaviours or have been subjected to them by others, and propose suggestions that I hope will help anyone navigating this landscape, as well as suggestions on policymaking and governmental controls I believe we should consider. However, I am not a psychologist or a medical professional, and I offer my thoughts as a researcher and writer invested in these issues, rather than as a provider of therapeutic guidance. I don't claim to have all the answers, but my hope is that the book's mix of personal stories, credible research and analysis of prominent ideas around our online world, as well as my experience as a digital strategist, will benefit those who are facing these tricky issues in their lives and are trying to navigate them.

Chapter 1 focuses on 'The Online Conspiracy Theorist': someone who may have said 'I read it online' a few too many times, using content that's not credible to justify an inaccurate belief. This chapter is about the confusing online sludge of conspiracy theories, hearsay and anecdote, which too often drowns out reliable and authoritative sources. The messy tangle of our information system has made seemingly reasonable people with real fears and uncertainties fall into patterns of conspiracy and radicalisation. Shining a light on the complex nature of how information spreads, ruthlessly designed algorithms and AI systems that prey on our doubts, as well as the malicious actors and naive adherents who spread misinformation, this chapter explores how difficult it is to get back to a shared sense of objective reality and a common understanding online – and how we need to issue life jackets for those prone to conspiracy theories.

Chapter 2 unpacks the psychology of 'The Freedom Fighter', who feels they have been treated unfairly by the government, civil institutions and laws that impose on the unfettered expression of their civil liberties. There is much uncertainty and injustice in the world right now, as we reel from catastrophe to catastrophe related to the climate, the pandemic, the economy, the geopolitical landscape. But we still operate in a society with laws and rules, and we still need a shared understanding of the social contract. Online, people who reject these rules can now come together at scale. Former fringe groups can connect and organise themselves to protest together. For freedom fighters, inconveniences become injustices, civility becomes censorship, and their perceived 'right' to freedom is paramount. This chapter shows how the global nature of the internet is causing chaos and how harmful ideas can spread quickly online, misleading people into thinking a world of self-expression is preferable to one that prioritises community safety.

Chapter 3 examines 'The Social Media Narcissist'. When our profiles on Instagram, Facebook and TikTok demand our 'best selves', there is a huge pressure to overexpose and overshare. In addition, the content-hungry feeds on social media reward the brightest, most picture-perfect versions of ourselves and our lives, and the dopamine hit we get from every like, 'heart' and positive comment can be intoxicating. Casual events become highly produced operations, life milestones become opportunities for photoshoots, random thoughts are turned into inspirational quotes and travel gives rise to an image library of curated clichés. When life becomes content and content becomes life, we turn into shallow narcissists who live for the likes. This chapter shows how this activity is not as new as it may seem, and suggests that the ability to build genuine connections and authentic relationships can be the antidote.

Chapter 4 looks at 'The Hateful Troll'. Why is it so easy to argue online? Why is trying to get across a thought, resolve a simple disagreement or come to a common understanding so difficult? The engineering of online platforms means so much is left unsaid that what results is an angry, disembodied back-and-forth where people who disagree can become hostile opponents and stop at nothing to get the last word. These fights can lead to real harms and victimisation, particularly for women, who disproportionately experience harassment and trolling online. By exploring how online platforms warp our ability to connect with one another and leave out a vast amount of communication information we need, this chapter suggests a sense of social boundaries and an intrinsic respect for others is vital when interacting online.

Chapter 5 swipes right on 'The Dating App Pest'. It's never been easier to get, give and have sex, thanks to the internet. 'The internet is for porn' became a popular saying because it displayed a simple truth – sex thrives online. With a dating app to suit every preference and proclivity, web apps and their offshoot, mobile apps, have opened up sexuality for millions of people. But this has also changed our relationships, our ideas of intimacy and our choices for romantic partners. *Tinderellas* and *Tinderfellas* choose from a menu of sexual partners and discard them just as easily. *Tinder swindlers* use online sites to trawl for vulnerable individuals to scam and defraud. Grindr enthusiasts treat other people as meat suits without emotions. This chapter unpacks how we are unable to relate to one another when even our most intimate moments and relationships are treated as commercial transactions, and how we can engage more authentically with others.

Chapter 6 logs on with 'The Screen Addict'. We now have a generation who don't know a world without the internet, and we are only at the beginning of a conversation about how to teach young people to use the internet responsibly. Because of smart devices, we have all inadvertently become gamers, as many websites and programs use game mechanics to keep us glued to our screens. What will it mean if we don't know how to disconnect? Will we produce a nation of addicts, unable to live without their devices, or must we simply learn how to adapt? This chapter explores the dangers of gaming and screen addiction while also demonstrating the surprising new benefits of playing, learning and living online.

Chapter 7 forecasts with 'The Naive Futurist' and looks at some of the macro technological trends coming our way – the metaverse, Web3 and more. A challenge in regulating our online landscape is that we continue to see our online selves as separate from our offline selves. This is, in large part, due to technology that keeps trying to replace or offer an escape from reality. This chapter maps out how technology is challenging our ideas of identity, reality and community in this new virtual space.

Finally, the conclusion reflects on the lessons of the book, reviews some reasons to be hopeful, and looks ahead for a new approach and narrative around how we relate to digital technology.

Why such a broad menu of internet-related issues? We need to develop a new, more holistic way of talking about the internet and the behaviours it can give rise to. Many of these personas are linked: the social media narcissist is likely also a screen addict; the freedom fighter is likely a conspiracy theorist and may be a hateful troll. The dating app pest might well feel pressure to be a social media narcissist to attract matches and, if they're a woman, is highly likely to have encountered trolls who abuse them online. These types give rise to discussion of a broad range of issues that share a fundamental commonality – they are facilitated, amplified and made worse by the current structure of the internet.

We know that the issues around internet use are real. We know that each story in this book represents thousands of people who have experienced online challenges. As with most complex conditions, there is an interplay of contributing factors. We cannot blame people for responding to algorithms, AI and gamification in the way the human brain is intended to. We also cannot excuse people for personal behaviours that extend to online hatred, abuse and the spreading of disinformation. With this in mind, I offer two types of recommendations at the end of each chapter. The first focuses on personal interventions – actions and initiatives individuals can take to increase their safety and behave responsibly online. The second looks at societal interventions – larger-scale proposals that need to be actioned at a company or government level, to create public good and systemic change when it comes to technology. A mix of the two is critical: we need interventions at both levels to create a heathier and safer online experience for all.

As noted, I am not a doctor or a therapist. I recommend seeking professional help for serious disorders. What I am is a researcher in internet communications, and I continue to see a lack of discussion around internet-related addiction and radicalisation, even as these conditions cause increasing harm. There is a grave lack of resources to help with much of what I write about in this book. Internet-related disorders are still often ill-defined within the medical community and not taken seriously. One clinician I spoke to for the chapter on screen addicts described being met with incredulity and confusion at a conference on addiction when he mentioned he focused on screen and gaming treatment. It is this persistent dismissal of the virtual that has led to a rapid proliferation of mental health issues and crises related to the internet. It is becoming a silent pandemic, and it needs more attention from healthcare providers, policymakers and the public. I have listed what helpful resources I could find in the 'Resources' section at the end of this book, but these are largely general in nature and not specific to online interventions. Still, they may provide a starting point for anyone seeking help.

Big Tech companies have a lot to answer for, and this book is for them, as well as for the governments who are trying to hold them to account, the members of the media who are trying to inform the public, the academics who are studying the effects of problematic internet use, and the critics who are trying to regulate the technology. But ultimately it is for the everyday people who are caught up in addiction, anger and radicalisation, and those around them. Change starts with just you and me.

1

The Online Conspiracy Theorist

Starting around 2016, millions of people around the world lost their minds.

It began in the United States. A pizza restaurant in Washington, D.C., became unexpectedly infamous when a rumour developed that its basement was being used to house and abuse kidnapped children. Then, as in a game of Telephone, the rumour grew: a cabal of politicians, business leaders and Hollywood elites were the ones abusing those children and draining their blood to create adrenochrome, a drug that promised immortality. Those who believed the rumour were crying out for something to be done to stop this horror. Who would put an end to it? Luckily, a hero emerged: word on certain message boards spread that Donald Trump, US presidential hopeful, was the saviour who would dismantle this heinous paedophile ring and bring the evildoers to justice.

Through the power of the internet, the rumour soon jumped countries, and Canadians and Europeans started posting about similar things. Then it reached antipodean Australia, where people from places like Reddy Creek and Chinderah, Ballina and Hobart – places as far away from American politics as you could get – started believing that

Donald Trump was a saviour of abused children … and also that 5G towers were spreading this new illness called coronavirus.

As 2020 lengthened and we officially entered the depths of a global pandemic, fear and uncertainty turbocharged people's receptiveness to conspiracy theories as we spent our days locked down, looking for answers and spending way too much time online.

The conspiracy theories that emerged during this period were diverse and multilayered, and were often adapted to focus on places and people close to home. Hollywood sex-trafficking tunnels morphed into storm-drain sex-trafficking tunnels beneath Melbourne; the list of those detained in the military prison Guantanamo Bay grew to include Victorian premier Dan Andrews, who became a target after strict lockdown rules; Australian 8chan users claimed a Sydney couple had been cured of Covid-19 after injecting disinfectant. Certain parts of the internet became a Petri dish of conspiracies about Covid-19, from the theory that it was created in a Wuhan lab to the idea that it could be cured by hydroxychloroquine to the suggestion that the pandemic was a hoax created by the liberal elite.

Much like Covid-19 itself, outlandish conspiracy theories continue to infect everyday Australians today. Unfortunately, these bogus theories are as real to those who believe them as Covid-19 is to the rest of us.

Conspiracy casualties and fake news fallouts

'She's gone … It's like she's there but it's QAnon speaking through her voice.' This is the anguished comment of a woman who watched her best friend become taken in by online conspiracy theories – and become so captive to the ideas of QAnon and other fringe groups that she no longer made sense to those around her. She was were struggling with the consequences of the phenomenon of internet radicalisation.

Most people in the grip of conspiracy are paranoid and suspicious, and so, unsurprisingly, are unwilling to speak to a researcher investigating the power of internet conspiracies. Try as I might to reach some of them, they labelled me a 'normie' (unenlightened person) who could never understand, or a 'glowie' (spy) who would get them in trouble. So instead I spoke with those closest to them, who were more than willing to have a sympathetic ear. I encountered a friend worried that she was the last connection to rationality for her QAnon-brainwashed loved one, a fed-up son who had cut ties with his conspiracy-obsessed mother for his and his family's sanity, and a loving partner struggling not be sucked into the rip of her partner's affliction.

Diana is the youngest of four sisters and grew up in a strict Christian family. Her father was a counsellor who worked with various groups, including those in aged-care homes and community centres. An anxious child, Diana found high school stressful and so, after a couple of years, her parents decided to try distance education. When this proved unsustainable for her too, it was decided she would be home-schooled. With her anxiety preventing her from interacting outside of the home, Diana became cut off from the wider world during a time when she should be most social – meeting different groups of people, exploring her likes and dislikes, finding her identity. Her father grew concerned that this level of isolation was not healthy, and so in 2018 he introduced Diana to Stacey.

Stacey was about Diana's age, an employee at an aged-care home studying to become a social worker. She was intelligent and sensitive, comfortable with herself, and had a community-minded spirit rare in older teens. She stood out to the counsellor in a facility full of retired, pensioner-aged residents and middle-aged workers. Diana's father approached Stacey and explained that he thought it would be helpful for Diana to spend time with someone as kind and well-meaning as Stacey, a 'good girl her age'.

Diana and Stacey soon became fast friends. They bonded over their shared love of animals, particularly horses, and their friendship centred on horseriding excursions. Diana loved to play with Stacey's old Jack Russell terrier. She dreamed of being a veterinarian. 'She was always much better with animals than she was with people,' Stacey reflected.

As Stacey got to know Diana, one thing stood out to her as a little odd – Diana loved to share conspiracy theories that she found online. It started slowly, as Diana tested Stacey's receptivity to her links and shares. Stacey humoured her. She knew Diana was sheltered and poorly socialised. Over time, Diana shared more and more stories with Stacey, and they became progressively more bizarre, from a blood-drinking elite cabal through to ritualistic slaughter. Evil, coded symbolism was hidden throughout the world, Diana told Stacey.

This pattern of progression is characteristic for many QAnon victims, as the conspiracies take hold of them and draw them deeper and deeper. They begin sharing a little with close friends and family, and gradually this escalates in frequency and bizarreness.

Stacey felt concerned about her friend but was unsure what to do about it. 'I started to worry when it seemed like she became unable to think for herself,' Stacey recalls. 'She went from calling flat-Earthers crazy to believing the Earth was flat because Q [the mysterious alleged leader of QAnon] told her it was. I realised her personality was becoming more of what Q and the commentators gave her rather than the "real" her.' She tried to refute Diana's claims with reason and logic, responding to Diana's clearly biased propaganda with credible, accurate information from reliable sources. But Diana would just find more content, from questionable websites and blogs, to respond with.

She didn't seem to understand that the sources of the information she was sending were not reputable.

Diana was an avid Trump supporter, even though, as an affluent urban Australian, she did not match the typical profile. But Diana's devotion to Q meant that she embraced everything Q said, including about the so-called leader of the free world. Over time, Stacey watched as 'it slowly became like Q was taking over her mind like a parasite'.

Diana became more and more paranoid, living in genuine fear of secret pedophiles, criminals and Satan worshippers. Q encouraged her to look for hidden symbolism everywhere – to find objects and text that bore signs of the shadowy, evil elite and their hidden machinations. Stacey describes how 'she would send me a picture of a (random) statue or art installation and point out how it's evil and how they use art as part of satanic rituals'. Parks and botanical gardens, or even plazas, which often have statues and artworks, became locations Stacey would avoid when they saw one another.

Because she lived in constant fear, Diana ventured out less over time, and she saw Stacey less and less often. Their outings turned from carefree adventures to tense meetings, which had to be held as close to Diana's home as possible. During the rare occasions that Diana and Stacey now went horseriding, Diana would check her phone every ten to fifteen minutes. These days, Diana and Stacey don't see each other much, but they text back and forth, their conversations almost entirely about conspiracy theories that run through Diana's mind.

When I ask Stacey why she has stayed friends with Diana, she answers defiantly, 'I'm the only (sane) person in her life now. If I leave, then she'll have no hope of ever getting away.'

———

Jarrod, a software developer in his thirties from Perth, had a long and painful journey with his mum before he decided enough was enough. The catalyst for his decision to cut her off was the birth of his child, which prompted him to think about whether it would be healthy for her to be around her grandchild.

Jarrod recounts how his mum, who is in her sixties, had always been 'an alternative type', into spirituality, wellness, alternative medicines and therapies: 'crystals and all that stuff'. She would 'never go with the grain'; she was 'unique that way', he says.

Jarrod helped his mother get connected to the internet, and he has no doubt that social media, particularly Facebook, was what exposed her to QAnon and sent her down a dark path. 'My siblings and I set up a Facebook page for her, and that was the real "jumping point",' he says.

Jarrod is clear about how the internet 'put petrol on the fire' of his mum's tendency to support ideas outside of the mainstream. Before she was online, she 'had to go to very specific places to find the books (and information)' related to her penchant for wellness and alternative therapies. But through Facebook, she got a direct line to these and more. Jarrod followed what she was posting on Facebook and witnessed the uptick in the frequency and intensity of her conspiracy-related postings. But it wasn't until 'it transitioned from being purely online … to the point where it became a regular topic of conversation in real life' that he really started to worry. Over dinner, at birthday parties and at events with friends and family, she would embarrass herself by being vocally pro-Trump, talking about the 'child abuser tunnel system' and 'baby blood drinking', which he had to 'explain [to the other guests] and apologise for after the fact'.

Early on, Jarrod tried the usual tactics to combat his mother's misinformation – reason, logical arguments, facts. But these were ineffective. Her conspiratorial beliefs married well with her outspoken, unapologetic personality, and she relished being different, 'the black sheep'. Jarrod's efforts at diluting her newfound passion seemed to her just another attempt to make her conform to the status quo, when she had built an identity around rejecting exactly that.

Jarrod realised that since her beliefs were not grounded in facts but in irrationality, it would ultimately be futile to try to refute them with argument. So he appealed to her sense of civility, pointing out that her behaviour was inappropriate and embarrassing those around them. That didn't really work either. As he grappled with how to gain traction with his mother, his reactions varied between stony silence and attempts at the 'grey rock method' – becoming unresponsive to the person's behaviour and words to avoid adding fuel to the fire – to anger and attempts at scolding her, which had the reverse effect, confirming her even more in her certainty. He even thought about cutting off her internet connection: 'I was thinking about how best to cut it [the disinformation] off from the source.'

As he sought to identify where online his mother was finding her information, he encountered an extensive network of social media influencers in the wellness community that she followed, all into 'healing', 'truth' and 'spirituality'. A particular icon was Patricia Cori, a septuagenarian 'spiritual leader' described in an online biography as 'an inspiring icon of truth and a living model of the adventurous spirit', who wrote books and created content based on her spiritual journeying. Her book titles read like a science-fiction catalogue: *The New Sirian Revelations: Galactic Prophecies for the Ascending Human Collective*, *Atlantis Rising: The Struggle of Darkness and Light* and *The Starseed Dialogues: Soul Searching the Universe*. The blurb on *The New Sirian Revelations* reads:

In July 1996, during an extraordinary out-of-body journey through the Milky Way and other galaxies, Patricia Cori was reconnected and attuned to a group of interdimensional light beings that she and her many readers came to know, through the first Sirian Revelations transmissions, as The Sirian High Council. During her remarkable mission as their Scribe, she has shared the insights of six-dimensional Sirian Light Emissaries through the books and teachings that have transformed readers over the past decades. Now, twenty years from the date of the first transmission, Cori shares new revelations that affirm the veracity of past prophecies and transmit new visions for the human race as we ascend through the outer reaches of the fourth dimension into new levels of conscious awareness and parallel realities as we prepare for our imminent emergence.[1]

One could be forgiven for thinking this is the plot of the latest Marvel film, but Patricia's fans, like Jarrod's mother, believe it completely.

Another key source was BitChute, a video hosting service that 'aims to put creators first' and allows them to 'express themselves freely' – which, perhaps inevitably, attracts far-right commentators and conspiracy theorists. His mother's interest in video content had started with YouTube, which introduced her to many of the main ideas of QAnon, and then she progressed to the more extreme and unfiltered content in BitChute.

Jarrod has actively sought support for his mother and for himself. He is well versed in the phenomenon of internet radicalisation and sensitive to its nuances. His experience highlights one of the most glaring difficulties for individuals confronting this problem in their families – there are few resources to help deal with this situation.

He feels like 'the right type of help' early enough may have salvaged the relationship with his mother but is unclear about what that help might have looked like, and he also acknowledges the difficulty in identifying the disorder early enough to employ this circuit-breaker. For his own wellbeing, he tried 'two or three different counsellors' but 'they couldn't really help much', given the specificity and the uniqueness of his circumstances. This sad lack of resources means that Jarrod was forced to try to help his loved one with little to guide him. While Jarrod is at peace with his decision to cut off contact, a rift between a mother and her son is always a sad thing.

Amy, a furniture maker from Melbourne in her forties, had no choice but to take up this challenge of finding help when her partner fell down the conspiracy rabbit hole. For her partner, the pandemic sparked an overwhelming sense of fear and anxiety that propelled her into the world of conspiracy theories, which 'provided (or appeared to provide) answers, certainty' and a grand design to the world's overwhelming and challenging problems.

'It started on Facebook during lockdown,' Amy says. She and her partner were usually busy and productive people, but the lockdown induced a new malaise and a sense of disconnectedness. 'There was not much else to do, she was bored, so she was on Facebook too much.' And the Facebook algorithm ushered someone who was looking for answers down a trail of disinformation, conspiracy and heresay.

Amy is vague about the period between the start of the issues and its lowest ebb, and I don't want to drill her on the details. Suffice it to say it escalated to the point where both she and her partner needed intervention. Amy's partner saw a psychologist and went on medication, while Amy tells me that, at her lowest, she asked doctors to 'put her in a coma', hoping to wake up when the pandemic (and her partner's affliction) had passed. When we speak, Amy tells me she has 'only just come off suicide watch'.

The enormous toll that it took on each of them was something the people around them failed to understand – a common theme among those suffering with loved ones in the grips of conspiracy. 'I couldn't talk to anyone about it, I couldn't talk to [my partner], our family didn't really get it, and some friends made it worse.'

For Amy, what the situation lacked was nuance. She felt that the pandemic had forced everyone to 'take sides' about Covid-related issues, such as vaccination, public health policy and mandates, topics that were at the centre of her partner's conspiracy concerns. This was mirrored by an online environment that drove polarisation and division among people. 'Online you are either on one side [of the conspiracy] or the other … I'm in the middle,' she says. Amy feels that this villainised her partner, who was coping with mental health issues. She is quick to defend her partner's intelligence, capabilities and mental curiosity. She couldn't see the villain that online commentators and the media described in this fragile, beautiful woman. This lack of nuance and compassion in public debate is a factor she blames for leaving those like her partner adrift. 'I had to make a choice, and I chose us,' she says.

Thankful for supportive friends and family, Amy now tries to balance out her partner's obsession with 'projects' and other forms of 'distraction' that help to keep her occupied and away from the internet. Filling her time with useful jobs around their community, gardening 'for the old ladies down the road', road trips and planning little escapes help to ensure outside influences beyond the all-consuming world of social media and the addictive virtual universe of conspiracy theories. Still, she acknowledges that her partner continues to feed this habit. 'She's on Telegram [an encrypted messenger service] a lot, and lots of chat rooms ... she checks the internet as soon as she wakes up at 4.30 in the morning.'

For Amy, the source of her partner's affliction could not be clearer. 'It started on Facebook, and YouTube as well.' She, like the other people I interviewed, wishes more than anything that this problem with social platforms would be taken seriously. In a voice cracking with emotion, close to tears, she says, 'No one is doing anything about this. This is a real issue, and no one is doing anything.'

QAnon – the ultimate online conspiracy theory

These stories are a snapshot of the problem of online radicalisation today. The accounts of online conspiracy theorists and their friends and families are baffling to those who have not experienced the phenomenon firsthand. And what many don't realise is that much of this outlandish disinformation starts with a shadowy character called Q.

Q's first appearance was on 4chan, an imageboard forum consisting of user-owned message boards, with a specific vocabulary and etiquette known only to its participants. The alias 'Q' was short for 'Q clearance' – a US Department of Energy status that allows for access to Top Secret restricted data. Claiming to be a US military intelligence officer, Q would post extremely short, vague and cryptic posts on 4chan and encourage anonymous users, or 'anons', to actively interpret the posts and try to make sense of them. Thus, 'QAnon' generated traction within the confines of 4chan's uber-online crowd.

What paved the way for Q was the conspiracy theory known as 'Pizzagate', which began in October 2016. Pizzagate centres on the widely discredited theory that Hillary Clinton was leading a child sex-trafficking ring out of the basement of a pizza restaurant in Washington, D.C. It emerged around the time of the US election, when Clinton was campaigning against Donald Trump, and many alt-right, conservative public figures happily spread the nonsense all over social media. A 28-year-old man from North Carolina was so disturbed that he went to the pizza restaurant to investigate the claims, firing shots with his AR-15–style rifle and threatening restaurant staff and customers. Although the theory has been debunked many times over, Pizzagate became a pillar of the QAnon phenomenon and evolved into a general conspiracy about powerful public figures, including Oprah Winfrey, Tom Hanks and Chrissy Tegan, allegedly participating in a vast network of child sex trafficking.

In 2017, 'Q Clearance Patriot', or Q, started posting on 4chan about a secret war happening unknown to the public. Q sent threatening, doom-laden posts about the ultimate war between good and evil, action against child-trafficking rings and 'true freedom'.

Observe the first Q post on 4chan in October 2017:

> HRC extradition already in motion effective yesterday with several countries in case of cross border run. Passport approved to be flagged effective 10/30 @ 12:01am. Expect massive riots organized in defiance and others fleeing the US to occur. US M's will conduct the operation while NG activated. Proof check: Locate a NG member and ask if activated for duty 10/30 across most major cities.[2]

'HRC' is Hillary Rodham Clinton, who was apparently planning to flee the United States. There is the threat of unrest, with claims the US Marines (M) and National Guard (NG) are ready for action. What made Q's posts enticing was the specificity of the predictions – actual dates and times were posted – and the air of real-world veracity: 'locate a NG member and ask if activated for duty …'. This made the content seem less like prophetic nonsense and more like actual dispatches based on real events. This first post set the tone of Q's alleged insider information, which often read like some sort of thriller.

A fundamental difference between Q and previous conspiracy theorists was the nature of online participation – the gamification, essentially, of each Q 'drop' or post. Q actively encouraged their audience to unlock the meaning of each drop's riddle, promoting crowdsourced analyses and interpretations of the 'code'. The suitably vague information in the drops facilitated open interpretation, like twisted horoscopes, as each person applied their own meaning and drew their own conclusions. Through the power of online networks, each of Q's drops strengthened the mythology around Q and drew more people into the game.

The Q drops that followed introduced Donald Trump as central to Q's grand theatre, a heroic figure bent on destroying the alleged elite cabal of villains and child-sex traffickers. It also introduced 'Operation Mockingbird', a supposed plot by the mainstream media to hide the crimes of the global elite. Thus the main players were established, with Trump and his supporters as the heroes and protagonists of the story, and liberals, Democrats, their supporters and the mainstream media as the villains.

Throughout 2017 the mythology deepened, as core slogans and terms for the group, such as 'the Great Awakening', were established. 'The Great Awakening' became one of the most popular catchphrases. It refers to a climactic event that will see Q's prophecies fulfilled. Other players and places were mentioned in this game, such as Huma Abedin, who was Clinton's political aide during her election campaign, and Barack Obama, John McCain, Iran and Saudi Arabia.

In 2018, Q moved from 4chan to 8chan (now called 8kun) following claims that 4chan 'had been infiltrated'. 8chan was similar to 4chan: an imageboard website made up of user-owned message boards. Many original users migrated after 4chan started to crack down on illegal or disturbing content, meaning that 8chan attracted the most extreme and radical users, who relished in its unregulated forums. It has been linked to white supremacism, neo-Nazism, extreme racism, antisemitism and severe hate speech. In 2018, Q also introduced the slogan 'WWG1WGA (where we go one we go all)', which took hold and further established the idea of QAnon as a unified movement. Some recognisable public figures, such as actor Roseanne Barr, also began to tweet in support of conspiracy theories linked with QAnon, such as the idea that Trump had 'freed so many children' from sex-trafficking rings.[3] Q drops during this time ranged from conspiracies about speakers having 'voice to skull' technology that brainwashes people, to conspiracies about deep state collusion with other countries. Q also 'predicted' a massive Republican win during the US midterms. As the election results came in showing the opposite, posts by QAnon followers foreshadowed the mood of the 2020 election, where Trump and his supporters claimed electoral fraud and voter interference.[4]

By mid-2019, QAnon had generated a significant public band of supporters, not the least of whom appeared to be the President of the United States himself, Donald Trump, who was repeatedly promoting accounts that showed support for QAnon on Twitter.[5] QAnon had exploded, becoming a popular movement with supporters all over the world. Many of its leaders profited handsomely from the movement, selling merchandise, books and videos, and became regulars on speaking circuits around the United States. Despite a string of failed predictions, the movement kept shifting the goalposts, with promises of more pivotal events to come and claims of coded messages within the failed predictions.

This complete denial of reality became an embedded feature within the QAnon phenomenon. Followers displayed acrobatic levels of cognitive dissonance and found ways to justify inaccurate predictions from past drops, perceiving any attempt to refute Q's claims as further validation of the 'conspiracy' working against them. Q's followers started to build an unbreachable alternate reality where they were free from failure and consequences.

Interestingly, around the time QAnon's followers grew worldwide, the influence of Q was starting to diminish. Their posts became more irregular and erratic. As the movement grew, its reliance on its figurehead declined: Q's culture of open interpretation and participation meant that individual followers could build upon any narrative thread they chose. QAnon became a many-tentacled octopus. As the cult's grand narratives around 'good versus evil' and active denial of facts became established patterns, followers felt free to co-opt any conspiracy or radical belief into the movement, and justified any opposition or fact-based debunking of it part of a broader move to 'hide the truth'. The nebulous nature of QAnon accommodated any believer who refuted facts, events and science in favour of their own unflinching delusions.

That year, three mass shootings – at a mosque in Christchurch, New Zealand; at a synagogue in Poway, California; and at a Walmart store in El Paso, Texas – were all linked to alt-right movements. The three shooters each posted their hateful manifestos on 8chan and announced their deadly intentions.[6] As the world reeled, in August 2019 8chan was taken offline, and remained so for several months. No Q posts were therefore circulated during this time. This hiatus was short, however, as the website reappeared, rebranded as 8kun, in November.

Cue 2020 and the deadly Covid-19 pandemic. As the world tried to grapple with the pandemic's health, social, economic and political effects, QAnon was also transformed, as it found new purchase and a raft of new conspiracies related to the pandemic. As we retreated into our homes and the internet became one of the only means of connecting and communicating with the outside world, internet platforms became a breeding ground for conspiracies, which emerged just as quickly and infectiously as the virus. Theories about 5G, hoax cures, labs in Wuhan, and the efficacy and effects of vaccines became fertile ground to attract new conspiracists. QAnon found an able partner in the wellness movement – sections of which questioned public health advice, preferred alternative therapies to science-based medicine and were already sceptical of vaccines.

Instagram 'influencers' who preached health and wellbeing represented an attractive new face of QAnon. Dubbed 'pastel QAnon', mummy bloggers, lifestyle coaches and wellness practitioners promoted inaccurate messages while posing glamorously and fed a hapless new audience raw conspiracies at a time when the world needed the exact opposite. This group of foolhardy social media enthusiasts were particularly drawn to the ideas around child-trafficking and child exploitation in early versions of QAnon, and they took up virtual arms against child abuse using the hashtag #SaveTheChildren. Many of their followers stumbled into a broader movement they knew little about, as confused parents and generally health-conscious people clicked on 'Save the children' content, not realising the name of the well-known aid agency was also the slogan of a dangerous conspiracy group that promoted violence and civil unrest.

The marriage between QAnon and the wellness movement demonstrated QAnon's capacity to meld concepts that were not even remotely connected into one amorphous pattern of belief. As clueless influencers created engagement bait, they projected baseless conspiracies and Q-adjacent theories to the broader public, spreading inaccurate beliefs far and wide. What started as essentially a treasure hunt or content puzzle for a group of fringe alt-righters hovering on message boards has grown to be something hugely complex: a confused, confusing, irrational web of mythology, conspiracy, misinformation, disinformation, political ideology and cult influences that has the capability to infiltrate a wide variety of psyches.[7] QAnon conspiracies have become so all-encompassing that 'QAnon' is now an umbrella term for a vast range of conspiracy theories, and many of its victims will not even realise that their specific beliefs were born within the QAnon phenomenon.

This is only a brief, potted history of QAnon – entire books have been written about it, exploring its origins, developments, precedents and impacts. There are other, smaller online conspiracy groups too. But QAnon is important because it has provided an online framework in which fringe ideas of all sorts can flourish. It facilitates irrational beliefs across theories worldwide. It has become self-sustaining and is often seemingly impermeable to outside influence. This is why the specific claims and predictions linked to QAnon early on, which were for the most part about American politics and American events, did not ultimately matter, and why its grip on followers is so strong – in its mess of predictions and conspiracies, it enables a kind participatory mass hysteria and fosters a self-reinforcing feedback loop of delusion.

The psychology of conspiracists

To understand why conspiracy theories take hold of certain people, we must first acknowledge a simple truth: some theories turn out to be true. Certain conspiracies have been proven, like the US government experimenting with mind control, the Dalai Lama being paid by the CIA to resist China, and powerful companies such as Big Tobacco covering up the harmful effects they cause. And intergovernmental espionage, shady corporate deals and undocumented corruption will continue to occur without the public's knowledge. The idea that those in positions of power and authority may abuse their influence is not baseless. Governments, large multinational corporations and powerful public figures can have inordinate, sometimes obscene, levels of wealth and influence. The notion that they may use this power against downtrodden, common folk is hardly far-fetched: history shows us that it happens regularly. A healthy distrust of the rich and powerful should be welcomed and is central for any free and functioning democratic society.

We also all harbour irrational beliefs of some kind, and if we were to openly admit to some of these, no doubt others might question those beliefs. What counts as rational to one person may seem irrational to another, religious belief being an obvious case in point. Sometimes, what may initially seem an irrational belief can be proven correct with time. Pioneering scientists with avant-garde ideas were labelled heretics and lunatics when they presented theories such as the Earth being spherical or orbiting the Sun.

Psychologist Rob Brotherton thinks people are all 'natural-born conspiracy theorists'. In his seminal book *Suspicious Minds: Why We Believe in Conspiracy Theories*, he suggests that '[c]onspiracy theories resonate with some of our brains' built-in biases and shortcuts, and tap into some of our deepest desires, fears and assumptions about the world and the people in it'. Rather than being a psychological aberration, they reveal how the human brain works.[8]

So when does a conspiracy theory become problematic? Mick West, a science writer and 'professional debunker', writes about 'the conspiracy spectrum', which encompasses a range of conspiracy beliefs ranging from what most people would consider plausible to the completely ridiculous. Where we draw the line between plausible reality and fiction is called the demarcation line. This demarcation line varies from person to person and group to group. Where conspiracies start to become problematic is when they become all-encompassing, particularly as those theories lean towards the more ridiculous end of the spectrum, and especially if they have been debunked.[9] We often refer to conspiracy theories as 'rabbit holes', of the *Alice in Wonderland* kind, as the conspiracy becomes a tunnel of all-encompassing belief until the conspiracist becomes cut off from the world they know and enters an alternative reality.

'Red pilling' is a term that many conspiracy theorists use today, derived from the science-fiction movie *The Matrix*. At a crucial point in the story, the protagonist, Neo, faces a choice. He must choose between a blue pill – which will return him to his 'normal' life – and a red pill, where he will be enlightened by the truth, awakened from his banal, programmed 'reality' into an apocalyptic but epic landscape where he becomes a hero in a titanic struggle between the forces of good and evil. Many conspiracy theorists laud this 'red pill' moment, when they were first exposed to a conspiracy theory. Most likely this took the form of a YouTube video, a post or group on Facebook, or a link from a questionable website, which begins their 'awakening'. As journalism professor Darlena Cunha explains the use of the term:

> If you take a red pill, your eyes are opened to the truth of the world, and you no longer exist in the prettier, but fake, world

you thought you lived in. If you take the red pill, you see the underpinnings of the world's networks, the push for power from various groups, the nefarious dealings of those in control to keep the masses satiated and at bay … there is a certain type of person who proudly proclaims to have taken the red pill most often. Men like Cesar Sayoc, the man who sent improvised explosive devices to critics of Donald Trump, and far-right conspiracy theorist and radio host Alex Jones. Men who hate feminism, who are against liberal ideas, men who believe in things like pizzagate, pick-up artists (PUAs), the manosphere (a group of online communities that include MRAs [men's rights activists], PUAs, incels and Men Going Their Own Way (MGTOW) among others) and QAnon.[10]

A number of studies have looked at the variables that may facilitate conspiracy thinking. French researchers Anthony Lantian, Dominique Muller, Cécile Nurra and Karen Douglas examined whether a belief in conspiracy theories satisfies a need for uniqueness. Their research found some causality between people's desire to be unique and their propensity to believe in conspiracy theories. As 'conspiracy theories represent the possession of unconventional and potentially scarce information', the higher on the conspiracist spectrum a person was, the more unique they considered their knowledge to be, and the more they tended to think of this as knowledge as difficult to acquire. In other words, they felt they were 'special', with access to secret knowledge few others had. A US study led by researcher Jack Edelson found that people are more prone to believe in conspiracy theories when they feel threatened or there is perceived risk, hence the prevalence of 'bad actors' and villains, including foreign agents and internal 'deep state' manipulators, among a raft of contemporary conspiracies.

University of Winchester psychology academic Mike Wood describes how conspiracy theories are most likely to arise during times of uncertainty, particularly if those events are personally threatening and directly relevant (an apt description of how things have felt for many during the pandemic).[11]

Overall, research suggests that conspiracy theories may appeal to people who wish to seek meaning about events that are of significance to them or carry meaning for them, but they face limitations that prevent them from finding the answers to their questions through more rational means. Some conspiracy theorists can be highly intelligent, but they construct the wrong patterns and fixate on erroneous concepts. In other instances, mental illnesses play a role. There are further correlations with suspiciousness, belief in the paranormal, narcissism, gullibility and lower media literacy, as well as rejection of conventional scientific findings.

Yet while conspiracy theorists can come in many forms, there is a very common pattern in the way many people today find and share conspiracy theories: online platforms. This crucial factor has not been given enough attention, or action.

'I saw it on YouTube', 'I read it on Facebook'

Of course, conspiracies have always existed. Of course, there are personality types that are more prone to conspiratorial thinking than others. Of course, the chaos and uncertainty of contemporary events have created ideal conditions for widespread conspiracy. And of course, there are bad actors willing to exploit these vulnerabilities. But it is important to note that QAnon, the mega conspiracy theory that has spawned many other conspiracy theories, is a thoroughly, fundamentally online phenomenon.

There is no denying that QAnon – the way it has enabled and facilitated other conspiracy theories, the way it fosters mass participation through gamification, and the way it went mainstream – was made possible by digital and social media platforms. Our 'always on' culture, the Big Tech business model of increasing and sustaining engagement, and the way social networks abuse our cognitive biases and tendencies have allowed online conspiracy theories to spread more rapidly, and to more people, today than ever before.

QAnon first originated in the swamps of 4chan, a haven for fragile and insecure young men. 4chan and its ilk attracted some of the worst, vilest elements of the internet, as the dark impulses of dysfunctional teenage boys and men angry at the world manifested in message boards and chats. But these were fringe communities, and largely stayed that way, too cryptic for the uninitiated and too impenetrable for the casual user. A turning point came when QAnon antics started getting noticed on Reddit, known as being 'the front page of the internet'. Reddit is a social media platform made up of 'subreddits', or forums with highly specific topics. Reddit is one of the original social networks and continues to be successful in part due to the degree of control it allows each community, with a culture of self-governance that is well understood by its participants. Reddit is significantly more mainstream than 4chan. It is getting increasingly popular, with corporate brands even attempting to penetrate its audiences.

Reddit became an important forum for bad actors who wanted to exploit the burgeoning movement that would become QAnon for their own gains. For instance, in 2016 a subreddit called r/Pizzagate attracted 20,000 subscribers in its first fifteen days. It was banned by Reddit's administrators because of threats posted against the group's perceived enemies. Many users who continued on the platform were vocal about what they saw as censorship. And many more became regular Reddit users, where they were drawn into other problematic subreddits with inflammatory content and false rumours.[12] Over time, this user base grew.

While Reddit continues to have its problems, it is one online platform with some degree of control over its products. Reddit has several features that ensure more governance over its communities than most other social platforms, including downvoting (voting a post down means fewer people will see it), karma scores (a low score usually means the community sees the user as a source of harmful or hurtful information) and human moderators. Together, these measures help to foster standards of behaviour in the platform. Users can downvote comments that are inappropriate, abusive or downright false until they disappear from view. Karma scores let people know whether the user is active and engaged or a grifter there to cause trouble. Each subreddit is policed by moderators, who set up specific and enforceable rules and have the power to ban or mute users. Communities within each subreddit largely respect these rules. So, while QAnon content appearing on Reddit was concerning, Reddit retained a degree of control.

The larger shift came when QAnon moved to the widely used social media platforms of Facebook and YouTube.

Facebook and YouTube, companies with modern-day Napoleonic ambitions, are available free of charge to anyone in the world with an internet connection. Whether through arrogance or naivety, Facebook and YouTube believe they can homogenise the experiences of everyone on Earth, with our diverse, myriad mix of cultures and histories, and create a single online community that suits everyone. Both companies embody a truly libertarian view of technology without borders, without constraints and without limitations. Ostensibly in line with that philosophy, they prefer to be hands-off when it comes to content moderation and information dissemination, claiming they are 'neutral' platforms.

But the real reason is that the companies that own these platforms want us to spend as much time as possible on their sites, regardless of whether the content we consume is harmful or not, so that we can see more ads. Both companies make their profits primarily by selling advertising. They need to maintain engagement at all costs, keeping users clicking on content and staying on their platform for as long as possible with minimal reason to leave. As a result, Facebook and YouTube have become viral content farms, addictive to the core, dispensing dopamine hits to the brains of every user.[13]

Moderating content at scale is costly, resource-intensive and challenging. This is part of the reason why Facebook and YouTube prefer to rely on machine-led moderation rather than employing human moderators.[14] As such, conspiracy theories thrive these platforms. As fast as one post or video is taken down in one part of the world, another is being shared somewhere else. Even worse, once these companies' algorithms determine you are interested in a certain topic, you will be bombarded with more of that same content. So if you are receptive or vulnerable to conspiracy theories, Facebook and YouTube will not only happily serve you this content, they will stuff you full of it every time you log on.

For many, Facebook and YouTube are the gateways that normalised and legitimised online conspiracy theories, making QAnon and their counterparts the global scourge we see today. 'The problem started with Facebook,' Amy recalls. 'It was Facebook that did this ... we've removed her [Amy's partner] from Facebook now, but the damage is done.'

So many stories I've heard or read describe how people first got introduced to conspiracy theories or had their 'red pill' moment on Facebook or YouTube. It is the most persistent thread I can determine in stories of falling down conspiracy theory rabbit holes, as users describe watching one video, then another, then another, until they fall deeper and deeper, trapped in an algorithmically curated tunnel. The mention of these two companies is so ubiquitous among those who research conspiracy theories that the point bears repeating: most recent conspiracy theorists began their obsession via YouTube or Facebook.

Large online platforms such as YouTube and Facebook deny their culpability in enabling conspiracy theorists, despite many stories from victims and their loved ones, and despite numerous credible studies into this phenomenon.[15] Even allowing for broad psychological factors such as personality type and a global climate of uncertainty, the single biggest risk factor for becoming a conspiracy theorist is exposure, and exposure is maximised in the curated landscape of social media. The algorithmically dominated, hyper-personalised world of social media networks are perfect hothouses for conspiracists.

Social networks also enable a strong social aspect to form around the spread of conspiracy theories, creating a sense of social validation and community for the conspirator. Jarrod describes his mother's obsession as a 'plugging of a social void' that has replaced her relative lack of real-life network, particularly as she increasingly alienates friends and family with her beliefs.

Although it began in fringe communities, QAnon found the ideal hosts for its virus, the perfect incubators, in Facebook and YouTube. The phenomenon of online conspiracists, a form of global mass hysteria, can only be controlled with stronger restrictions on content, including around algorithms, on such platforms. And we need digital and real-world interventions for those who are caught in tunnels of disinformation, as well as greater support for those have no choice but to try to lure these loved ones out of their rabbit holes all on their own.

Finding a way out of the rabbit hole

In June 2021, *Mashable* published an article by journalist Rebecca Ruiz with an apt headline: 'Conspiracy theories are a mental health crisis'. An obsession with conspiracy theories may not be a clinically diagnosable disorder – yet – but it has affected many individuals. Families and friendships have been broken by this phenomenon, which on all available evidence has accelerated rapidly during the pandemic.

These mental health effects are symptomatic of a wider crisis. As Ruiz notes, 'It's becoming increasingly clear that without efforts to meaningfully address people's mental health needs, before or after they become deeply involved in conspiracy theories and disinformation, we'll make little progress toward defeating the dishonesty that pollutes our dialogue and discourse.'

We are still to determine the full extent of the effect that social media and other digital platforms have on us as a society. There are even those who go as far as comparing social media platforms to cults, such as Dr Steven Hassan, a cult deprogramming specialist. Hassan notes that ultimately social media and cults share the same underlying goal – to influence people, often to their own detriment. Influence is a continuum: some attempts at influence, such as positive reinforcement, contribute to healthy outcomes, while others, such as coercion and manipulation, are destructive. Social media falls on the unhealthy side of this spectrum.[16]

Like Big Tobacco and Big Oil before it, Big Tech promotes the narrative that its companies have a benign, positive influence in society.

Importantly, these companies put much of their energy into sustaining this narrative, focusing on new developments in technology and new phases of the web, instead of accounting for their mistakes or offering support to those affected negatively by their platforms. But the message from victims is loud and clear – this needs to be taken more seriously, and more resources and support are essential.

What can individuals do?

Decide if you want to intervene

Most people in the grip of conspiracy theories will resist any form of intervention. Some experts even advise against trying to reason with those far down the rabbit hole, such as journalist Mike Rothschild in his book *The Storm Is Upon Us: How QAnon Became a Movement, Cult, and Conspiracy Theory of Everything*. There is evidence that this may have an adverse effect, forcing the conspiracist to dig in their heels and strengthen their irrational beliefs further. The well-known 'backfire effect' theory (though it is not universally accepted) holds that when a person has their opinion or belief contradicted by facts, instead of their worldview changing, they become more set in their opinion. This is an innate cognitive bias, some argue, as our brains look to simplify and streamline competing information.[17]

There's a reason why the case studies I presented come from those who are closest to the conspiracist – they are the ones who have tried to help or are still willing to try to rehabilitate the person they love. And it is this type of consistent, gentle effort that is required to help someone start to question their conspiratorial beliefs and their irrational behaviours. Some people may not want to be rehabilitated. Some are probably too far down the rabbit hole, and will stay that way for a long time, if not forever. Others may find their way out of their own volition, given the space and support to work it out for themselves. But it may take years, or a suitably disruptive event to force some sort of reflection that may spark a broader questioning of the conspiracies which have taken hold of their lives.

It is important, then, to ask a question upfront: do you really want to take the time, effort, energy and patience to intervene in a loved one's deep belief in online conspiracy theories? It will likely take a personal toll on you as well, so you must be prepared.

If you do want to intervene, spend some time thinking about your own limits: how far will you go to help this person? Is there a point at which you would cut off contact, for the sake of yourself and others in your life? While these are not simple questions, developing some clear parameters about what you will and won't accept in terms of another's behaviour and its impact on your life can help you to make sense of the situation and guide your actions.

Look for the root cause

We know that most people who become devoted conspiracists get an emotional payoff from their irrational beliefs. Try to understand as much about their situation as you can: the nature of the conspiracy they believe in, the extent of its hold on them, their reasons for being attracted to it to begin with, and their reasons for continuing to believe it – what intangible benefits is it giving them? They may have certain personality traits that have made them more susceptible to conspiracy theories, such as a desire to feel special, or they may be battling with anxiety and fear, so the apparent rationality of these irrational beliefs is comforting. They may be lonely or disconnected in their offline lives, and so enjoy spending time in a welcoming online fellowship. Finding ways to address these root causes may have the effect of lessening the individual's reliance on their irrational beliefs. For instance, Amy encouraged her partner to reconnect with her local community to reduce her pandemic-induced sense of isolation.

In many cases, a formal intervention is needed. The trouble with QAnon-related addictions is that the condition is still relatively new and very specific. Jarrod approached three therapists, none of whom he felt could provide him much in the way of guidance. Amy and her partner found better luck with psychologists who could help address some of the root causes, but some addiction remains. Stacey suggested that the only intervention that might work for Diana is a cult specialist or 'deprogrammer' like Dr Hassan – this industry is of course unregulated and has potential dangers. There needs to be significantly more investment in resources and research around mental health and addiction in relation to conspiracies. Yet professional counsellors or psychologists may help some with addressing and managing the condition and some of the elements that surround it – such as social isolation, feelings of helplessness and depression, and anxiety. A general practitioner or the Australian Psychological Society's 'Find a Psychologist' service are good places to start in seeking professional help.

For those supporting a conspiracist, it may be helpful to connect with others who are going through a similar situation, to talk through and share experiences. Grassroots and community-driven support groups are popping up online for those who are proactively seeking to understand their loved one's changed behaviour and to intervene to set them on a healthier course. Groups like the subreddit /QAnonCasualties, which was established to offer 'support, resources and a place to vent' for those who 'have a friend or loved one taken in by QAnon', may be a helpful resource to connect you with others in similar situations.

Engage in good faith

It can be difficult to engage with someone whose views may seem so fundamentally different from yours, or who appears irrational and nonsensical. But if your words are to have any impact, it is essential to engage in good faith.

Engaging in good faith means being genuinely open and willing to understand another's point of view. It means being respectful of it, not deriding or mocking it. This does not mean agreeing with a belief you do not – it is about creating a safe and non-judgemental environment where the other person feels they can share their thoughts with you.

Engaging in good faith may mean that you are prepared to genuinely make an effort to understand, or at least gain a working knowledge of, their beliefs. In the confusing sludge of topics and branching logic around QAnon, for instance, it may help to have a basic understanding of the movement's major themes and stories – Pizzagate, the idea of a cabal of elites seeking to control the world and harm our children, and the 'libertarian' bent of dismantling institutions to facilitate individuals' freedoms, whether it's the political system, the media, public health institutions or elements of civil society. These themes can provide you with anchor points amid the otherwise obsessive specificity that can dominate conversations. The aim is to develop sincere communication and begin a dialogue. A conspiracist needs to believe that you are a friend, even if you do not subscribe to their obsessions.

It's also worth remembering that, most often, conspiracists have genuine fears that have led them to adopt irrational beliefs. Being empathetic to these concerns helps to build open communication. It's easy to understand that a parent might be concerned for their children's health and sceptical of new treatments or remedies. It's perfectly reasonable for someone who has been treated harshly by authorities in the past or is from a marginalised group to believe that those in power don't have their best interests at heart. But when those concerns lead to bizarre conclusions about drinking bleach or lizard people, logic has left the building. Focusing on a conspiracist's rational concerns rather than their irrational conclusions will help you to find common ground.

If you believe strongly in a conspiracy theory, you may feel that those you care about have been tricked, are being fed incorrect information, or simply don't know as much as you do. It can feel like there is an imperative to educate or even to warn them. Offer others the usual courtesies of good-faith engagement: allow them to express their thoughts and the reasons for their way of thinking. Openness of communication and exchange of ideas needs to go both ways.

Communication is crucial to the health of any relationship. Often conspiracy theories become all-encompassing and dominate the conspiracist's thoughts and daily life. A healthy relationship means that you're able to speak on a range of topics and find common ground on subjects not just about conspiracies. Whether you are deeply involved in conspiracy theories or supporting someone who is, remember to discuss other things: shared hobbies or interests, mutual friends, the children and pets in your lives. We all need a funny dog story sometimes.

Know that time is key

If you do want to have those conversations with a loved one – or if you recognise your own behaviours in the content of this chapter – it is important to remember that worldviews don't change overnight. Just as the path into conspiracy likely took some time, so too will any transition away from it. Any progress in thought away from conspiracy theories may come in messy bursts, fits and starts, or in cycles. There are no clear rules in trying to disentangle someone from ideas and systems that are by nature addictive and self-reinforcing. There are also potential dangers in trying to move too quickly: replacing one set of problematic behaviours with another set that is just as destructive is not good for anyone. You may not know when an epiphany or an opening could happen. It could occur unexpectedly, and when it does, you can be ready to seize the moment and engage.

Disconnect from YouTube and Facebook

As we have seen, YouTube and Facebook are hothouses for conspiracy theorists and may be the single biggest enablers of casual conspiracy theorists globally. A temporary or a permanent break from these platforms may be the single most helpful thing an individual can do. It's a good idea to remove yourself from the source.

Of course, YouTube videos are embeddable across the internet, and you can easily find them in other websites apart from the platform itself – and even embedded videos can sometimes promote suggestions for what to watch next based on your watch history. With a conspiracist in the grips of addiction, this is often enough to propel them back into the arms of the algorithm, as they find themselves seeking out and clicking on video content that should be a red flag. For such people, a temporary break from online browsing altogether may be warranted.

Conspiracy theorists are also now gathering in private settings – through apps such as Telegram and on private chat services. If someone wants to be part of these discussions, they will find a way. But preventing casual encounters with conspiracies and their proponents on Facebook and YouTube may be a worthwhile first step. In addition, sometimes other relationships may propel a person into conspiracism, so blocking, muting or unfollowing any such friends, and unsubscribing from certain groups, can also be helpful.

Employ debunking techniques

There are mixed views on whether debunking works with conspiracy theorists. When a belief is not grounded in logic, discrediting it with logic is often ineffective. Further, some feel that this creates a situation where someone has to win and someone has to lose, so both sides become combative, and this dynamic is not conducive to behaviour change.

Often, conspiracy theorists become fixated on very specific details that they feel validate their beliefs or reveal a grand design, when an impartial observer might see nothing but a random set of data. Psychologist Steven Taylor suggests that 'conspiracy theories are resistant to falsification in that they postulate that conspirators use stealth and disinformation to cover up their actions, which implies that the people who try to debunk conspiracy theories may, themselves, be part of the conspiracy'.[18] In other words, if you try to correct a conspiracist's erroneous belief through logic, they may simply dismiss you as a 'shill' (a disingenuous or inauthentic person who doesn't believe what they preach), thus damaging your chances at trying to get through to them.

Still, in this confusing and persistent phenomenon, we cannot say for sure what will work for a particular individual. Mick West, a 'professional debunker' for more than a decade, offers techniques that he claims to have used successfully with hundreds of conspiracy theorists.

- **Supplying useful information.** This can include correcting errors – if a conspiracy theory is not complex, a simple explanation or the provision of proof can correct that error, such as showing a historical photograph or a news report of what actually occurred during an event. It can also include discrediting their source. Facebook and YouTube lure in potential conspiracists as they also host news stories and information from credible media organisations and research institutions. But discrediting a particular website, article or video by demonstrating that other content it presents is incorrect could be effective with some.

- **Spotlighting.** This involves shining a light on a specific claim and marshalling the evidence against it. West gives the example of the chemtrail conspiracy theory (a theory that posits trails of chemical or biological agents sprayed for generally immoral purposes). One of the most common beliefs is that contrails – vapour trails from aircraft – cannot persist for more than a few minutes, so anything that lasts longer must be a 'chemtrail'. West has debunked this claim on his website *Contrail Science* by collating scientific information from '70 years of books on clouds and weather', as well as a series of historical photographs, which all demonstrate that contrails can persist for a long time under the right conditions.[19]

- **Floodlighting.** This technique is about debunking theories through sheer weight of evidence. Often those who believe in conspiracies suffer from 'crippled epistemology', meaning they have a narrow and restricted set of information sources. Floodlighting may be effective against this. Many conspiracy theorists have encountered counterarguments for their most common claims, but floodlighting goes one step further and captures the evidence against *all* their claims. Often the specialist nature of the topics prevents would-be debunkers from engaging, given the time required to detangle the overwhelming detail associated with each conspiracy theory. But for those who are serious about intervening, floodlighting may be a way to get that person to start questioning their own beliefs.

Dr Steven Hassan has developed the BITE model of authoritarian control, 'BITE' standing for Behaviours, Information, Thoughts and Emotions. The model looks at mind control and draws on research from brainwashing experts and cognitive dissonance theory to describe specific methods and techniques that cults use to maintain control over people. It describes methods such as regulating diet, controlling appearance, dictating how and when the individual interacts with family and friends, minimising or narrowing information sources, compartmentalising information into Outsider vs Insider doctrines, misquoting or manipulating outside information, instilling black-and-white thinking, creating false memories or information, and offering extreme emotional highs and lows – many of which have clear parallels with how the digital platforms of today work, if you think about it. Like spotlighting or floodlighting, the BITE model may provide more clarity and definition around the specific techniques that are prompting behaviour changes and compliance.

What can governments and society do?

Develop and invest in treatment and rehabilitation

The DSM-5, the *Diagnostic and Statistical Manual of Mental Disorders*, is the most widely used benchmark for mental health disorders globally. While its list of conditions is extensive, there are no listings for online conspiracy-related disorders. The closest reference is to 'internet gaming disorder', which is described as a condition that needs further study.[20]

As this problem grows to affect more individuals and their families, we need services that can deal specifically with conspiracy thinking and other problematic online behaviour. Governments and private institutions need to invest in expanding the research base and funding around these topics so that we can develop targeted, clinically sound interventions. It is woeful that online conspiracism isn't being treated as the serious condition that it is. We must spend significantly more on its study, research, treatment and prevention to help those afflicted by it.

Hold YouTube and Facebook to account

The role which YouTube and Facebook play in facilitating and amplifying conspiracy theories is clear. Research points to the fact that YouTube and Facebook's quagmire of content, their hands-off approach to content moderation and the sheer scale of their global user base means that they are key incubators for conspiracy theories.[21]

These platforms should not be allowed to keep denying their culpability. Governments, policymakers, the mainstream media, civil society, academia and every sensible institution that can influence the conversation must push to hold YouTube and Facebook to account for their social harm. Public pressure and, importantly, legislation are the only levers that will make these tech giants react. There have been some attempts at regulation in Australia – notably the *Online Safety Act 2021*, which goes some way towards delivering the needed protections. But many government measures have been woefully ineffective, such as the voluntary Code of Practice for Disinformation and Misinformation, which is essentially a tick-box exercise.

It isn't even unreasonable to suggest that platforms should pay some form of compensation for the social harms they cause through their content. Like oil companies that must pay economic damages to those harmed by a spill, why shouldn't technology companies be penalised for allowing inflammatory, violent and malicious content to spread across our community? These funds could be used to help those seeking treatment for conditions such as online conspiracism. Such an idea might sound radical, but it would ensure that these platforms have a vested interest in monitoring their content.

Create a minimum standard of care and safety for all online and social media platforms

As regulators grapple with how to make our online experience safer, one recurring concept is to create a minimum standard of care across all online and social media platforms. The UK Department for Digital, Culture, Media and Sport has proposed a statutory duty of care on online platforms as part of its Online Safety Bill. It is targeted at those platforms that host or publish user-generated content and requires them to put in place systems and processes that limit harmful or illegal content. The proposed legislation outlines significant penalties and fines for any company found to be in breach.

While the bill has attracted some controversy, the idea of a legislated safety standard to protect users is welcome. A duty of care forces responsibility and accountability standards on Big Tech companies, which have historically been too lax in their responsibilities to moderate and remove content and have often only acted to resolve issues on their platforms once the damage has already been done.

Standards of safety have long been in place for industry, such as the pharmaceutics and automotive sectors, as well as within public services. Given the outsized influence and impact of online platforms, it makes sense that this safety mindset be required for online companies as well.

Teach the community about credible sources

Many of us are not critical enough of the content we encounter online. If we come across an article, link or idea on a widely used platform such as Facebook or YouTube, we may assume it must be true. Those who are online-savvy are more likely to look at the source of the information: is it from a respected news organisation or a peer-reviewed journal? Is it written or created by someone with authoritative credentials – for example, an academic at a university or a journalist at a major newspaper? If they get as far as reading the piece or watching the video, they will also be more likely to evaluate the quality of its content. For example, does it contain objective facts and verifiable citations, or does it rely on hearsay and anecdote? Is its tone fair and balanced, or does it employ persuasive language techniques that sensationalise or promote conflict? What criticisms could be made of its argument?

These critical-thinking skills and content-vetting practices should become second nature for everyone in our content-saturated world. They should be taught in every school subject – not only in English or History classes, but as part of any school assignments that involve internet research. They should be incorporated into community courses about how to use the internet or made part of the free resources available at public libraries and community centres. A checklist of these sorts of questions should be posted at every computer terminal in every public, university or school library. It should be in the welcome screen when a user logs onto the free wi-fi.

Building a collective understanding of what constitutes credible information may help to minimise the number of people who become drawn in by conspiratorial content, and it may help others to recognise these signs in those around them earlier on. Such measures are important to ensure that people are regularly questioning information they come across online.

———————

Our complex information ecosystem will only get more sophisticated over time, and the number of digital platforms will only increase. Do we want to build the kind of online world that leaves in its wake confused conspiracists? Or do we want to create an environment that is dependable and healthy, with built-in safeguards for those who are most vulnerable to being pushed to extremes? We all know the future we prefer, and we must work together to bring it about.

The Freedom Fighter

A friend of ours almost ruined Christmas. On 24 December 2021, my partner got told that his regular swimming buddy had tested positive for Covid-19. It turned out he knew he was a close contact of another positive case only days before, but he still chose to spend time with my partner.

I was furious, incredulous, aghast. Even as the Omicron strain ripped through New South Wales after the state government's haste to ease restrictions, I had continued to be vigilant when it came to mask wearing, handwashing, social distancing and risky behaviour overall. Not only did I not want to get Covid, but I didn't want to pass it on. I was thinking about my father, who has type 2 diabetes and is in his late sixties. I was thinking about my newborn niece who, at two weeks old, had virtually no immunity to pretty much anything.

I confronted this friend. I told him that I was angry he had been irresponsible, and I asked for an explanation. To his credit, he accepted my reprimand. His explanation, however, continues to baffle me. He believed that the population of New South Wales had reached a level of vaccination where the specifics of Covid-19 management, including the instructions around what to do if you're a close contact, were guidelines rather than rules. He had a fatalistic attitude – we'd all get Covid-19 eventually, was his line of thinking – so to him, the rules did not matter.

For this friend, the health advice was open to interpretation. The rules were an imposition on his freedom and so he chose to believe he did not have to follow them.

I still do not understand this way of thinking. The experience led me to explore how apparently rational, ordinary people could take this mindset to more extreme and more aggressive applications than my partner's friend – to protests and violence. What would it take to jump from seeing health restrictions and public health orders as inconvenient to seeing them as something to rebel against?

What were the protests about?

The first evidence of lockdown fatigue and aggression was seen during the early days of the pandemic. In April 2020, as much of the United States was locked down due to skyrocketing Covid-19 cases, protests across the land of the free attracted thousands who wanted to 'reopen' the country. President Trump incited many by calling to 'liberate' certain states from lockdowns.

Anyone who has experienced a lockdown can identify with the feelings of frustration and anger it can give rise to – it's difficult to have to change your daily routines so radically, and to be separated from friends and family. But this wasn't a spontaneous, uncontrollable outpouring of public rage. Influential forces fanned the flames of protest. In many cases, these influences wanted to remain hidden. Many protests were organised by political operatives using social media and websites to encourage people to rail against governments and leaders who imposed strong public health restrictions. Investigations showed that domains for several related anti-lockdown websites and social media groups were registered to a small number of people who clearly wanted to spark unrest. They were linked to white supremacy groups that wanted to exploit the chaos and uncertainty of the pandemic to further their agenda for civil war and racial conflict.[1] Many who ended up participating in the protests likely never realised that they were being manipulated by those who wanted to mobilise their feelings of rage to attack political opponents and enemies.

Importantly, these protests, intended to target specific political figures in the United States, spawned copycat protests elsewhere that were almost entirely divorced from the political landscape in which they were taking place. Ideas that were uniquely American around state militias and the right to bear arms spilled over to hapless populations elsewhere as disembodied ideologies were shared online without context or local relevance.

It didn't matter that the sources and the motivations were different – the anger and frustration were real, and they could be exploited. Over the coming months and years, there were protests in places such as Poland, Brazil, France and Germany, with hundreds of participants, leading to many fines and arrests. In Brussels, the capital of Belgium, there were protests over the Covid pass, which restricted entry to bars and restaurants for the unvaccinated. Protestors threw fireworks at police, who retaliated with tear gas and water cannons. In the Netherlands, protests escalated into violence over several nights following lockdown orders.[2]

In Australia, public protests started in Melbourne. They targeted Victorian premier Daniel Andrews, who imposed several lockdowns, which eventually led to Melbourne gaining the unenviable title of one of the most locked-down cities in the world. There were several 'Freedom Day' protests throughout Australia in 2020. Thousands also gathered in Sydney in 2021, chanting 'Freedom!' and holding up signs with slogans such as 'Drop your mask, raise your voice' and 'Wake Up Australia' as states reimposed lockdowns to halt the accelerating spread of the Delta variant.

Protests continued throughout 2021, in capital cities and regional centres. One of the more violent occurred in Melbourne in September 2021, when the Victorian government decided to suspend work on construction sites for two weeks and make vaccination mandatory for construction workers. The Victorian Construction, Forestry, Maritime, Mining and Energy Union (CFMMEU) headquarters was stormed by a furious crowd, including many far-right protesters. Several officials confirmed that the protests were hijacked by far-right and anti-vaccination groups, and that only a small minority of the protesters were legitimate construction workers who would have been affected by the mandates.[3] Bizarrely, there were also protests from frontline healthcare workers who opposed vaccine mandates, including many nurses. In New South Wales, protests led to the arrest of key organisers. By the end of 2021, Australian authorities were well prepared and police were deployed in force for any planned protests. Many failed to gain traction, and some attracted only a smattering of attendees, where protesters were almost outnumbered by police.

Late January and early February 2022 saw a copycat protest based on the 'Freedom convoy' demonstration in Canada, where a group of anti-government, anti-vaccine truckers created a blockade, attempting to impede vital US–Canada border crossings. Australia's version, a 'convoy to Canberra', attracted anti-vaxxers, self-proclaimed 'sovereign citizens', ultra-religious groups and even members of Clive Palmer's United Australia Party. These disparate clusters found common cause – in much the same way as QAnon absorbed other conspiracy theories into its fold, the anti-vaccination 'freedom' movement became a rallying point for a range of special-interest groups. Many organisers and participants were there for the Millions March against Mandatory Vaccination protests, but there was also a motley collection of confused allegiances among the crowd, including some who claimed to be demanding rights for Indigenous people, despite representatives of the Aboriginal Tent Embassy clarifying that the lockdown protestors were not connected to their cause. There were also conservative Christians who performed baptisms along the drive to Canberra and blessed the grounds of the protests. As a blockade, it was a pale imitation of the Canadian version, with caravans and family four-wheel drives dominating. The protestors were largely opposing vaccine mandates but also had a 'hodge-podge of other grievances', including ending restrictions, protecting children, capturing paedophiles and removing Scott Morrison.[4]

What they all wanted was 'freedom' – although it was hardly clear or consistent what they meant when they invoked that term. For some, it meant freedom from government-imposed mandates; for others, it was freedom from vaccines themselves; and for others still, it was freedom from political and public institutions, and a desire to live by their own rules as 'sovereign' citizens.

Local Canberrans and public figures were rightly frustrated at the hostile takeover of their city. Many mocked and belittled the protestors, dismissing their concerns. And while more than a few of the grievances voiced may have been spurious, among the crowd there were some who had experienced real pain and hardship during the long years of the pandemic. These people felt they had been pushed to the brink, and their cries of 'freedom' contained a note of anguish.

'We've had enough'

Scott, twenty-six, was a disability support worker for high-needs children with autism. He had been with the same company for almost seven years when the Delta wave hit Australia.

During the first wave in 2020, with the Alpha and Beta variants, Scott was chosen to be the Covid-19 marshal for his local office in the Illawarra region. He happily undertook the training for this, as he felt it added extra value to his role. His impasse with the company came in 2021, during the second wave. By this point, vaccinations had become a central feature of the public health response. Being vaccinated was a requirement to visit public places, such as cafes, shops and entertainment venues. Scott refused to get vaccinated, but he was still able to work at the centre where his disabled clients lived. However, his ability to perform his duties was stymied by the fact that he couldn't take his clients out to public areas where vaccinations were required. Then new public health orders came into effect in his state: disability support workers were required to be vaccinated by 25 October 2021. As he continued to resist being vaccinated, Scott was told that he wasn't going to be able to work at the company anymore. 'I was shoved out the door without so much as a thank you after seven years.'

Scott's reasons for resisting the mandate were around 'medical privacy' and 'freedom of choice'. He told his employer that he did not wish to disclose his overall health status. He framed his reluctance to them by explaining that 'it's not normal to go around asking [someone] about their medical history and health status', including their vaccination status, and he believed that should apply here as well. He also recoiled at the compulsory nature of the public health advice: 'It's never been compulsory for me to get the flu shot, but all of a sudden, this [Covid-19 vaccine] was.'

Scott tells me that he knew of adverse reactions to the Covid-19 vaccine and wanted his employer to give him extra protections should he have such a reaction. He cites two incidents – a former colleague who he said was hospitalised due to the vaccine and a friend who had an AstraZeneca jab, 'got a blood clot and dropped dead two days later'. Scott said these cases were a major factor in his decision to go against the mandate. His employer refused to grant the requested protections because it was a government-led public health mandate. He felt he had alternatives to working for a company that was 'forcing' him to do something he wasn't comfortable with and chose instead to embrace a relaxed, semi-nomadic life in his campervan: 'just go travelling and surf'.

Scott's ultimate argument against vaccines is 'personal choice'. He baulks at being forced to do things that infringe on what he believes is a right to choose 'however [people] want to live their lives'. He claims he hasn't attended any lockdown protests but says he was extremely supportive of the 'people speaking out'. Scott's style of protest was more individualistic: he preferred to 'sit on the sidelines' as the people who were against the government mandates duelled it out with the government. He says friends who protested were sought out by police. The caginess he expresses has been mirrored in other conversations I've had, as some have accused me of being a 'glowie' – a covert operator working for the authorities who seeks out lockdown protestors with hopes of getting them in trouble.

When we discuss his background, Scott tells me he was raised in a 'generally conventional way'. His family are all vaccinated. His eldest sister is a science teacher and another is a nurse. He recalls 'getting a lot of pressure' to go to university after doing well in school. Following three years of uni and realising it would 'lead to mostly a desk job', he decided he didn't want to do that – he 'just wanted to go surfing' and travelling. He credits this epiphany as leading him to his mostly alternative views, including on vaccination.

Scott also recognises the impact that social media platforms have had on his views. He says they force people into more radical manifestations of their beliefs. With daily checks of Instagram and Facebook, mostly to stay abreast of his network, he says he's had to back off these platforms as 'it gets too full on'. He followed certain pages and profiles, like Reignite Democracy Australia, social media 'influencer' Primod and One Nation senator Malcolm Roberts, but says the platforms then barrage you with dozens of other similar profiles. He feels this amplifies his interest in anti-vaccination views and can serve to indoctrinate users into more extreme levels of engagement. He must regularly check himself when he feels he 'gets too involved', as he can fall down social media rabbit holes that are 'never-ending and infinite'.

Scott recognises the reality of Covid-19 and even followed isolation orders when he got the Omicron variant during the Christmas 2021 holidays. He was concerned for his family, whom he had visited days before, and especially for his sister's newborn. He 'wanted to do the right thing' and was concerned he would get really sick given he is unvaccinated. 'Just because I'm not vaccinated doesn't mean I want everyone else to get it.' Scott's resistance was mostly about the 'freedom of choice' against mandates and public health orders. For others, it ran much deeper.

––––––––––

Kylie's pain is barely contained and comes through in her voice. The pandemic turned her life upside down and the trauma it caused her was palpable. As the pandemic rolled through, her work dried up virtually overnight, leaving her without an income. Multiple lockdowns and the uncertainty of the pandemic destroyed her employment prospects as the casual work she did – driving, logistics and manual labour – stopped.

Despite applying and qualifying for various government assistance grants, she barely received any money, and to this day she doesn't understand why. Once the temporary moratorium on rental evictions ended, she was kicked out of her apartment. Her relationship couldn't take this strain and her partner left. At forty-five, she found herself jobless, homeless and alone.

Kylie says she has always been 'awake' but the pandemic escalated things. As she tried to make sense of her disintegrating world, she found Q, and she found 'the truther and freedom movement'. There is conviction and a certain poignant truth to her words when she declares, 'When you lock people up without any support, without any hope, what do you think they're going to do? They're going to revolt.'

Kylie is most compelling when she's reflecting on her personal situation, but for the most part she jabs at me verbally with the staccato monologue of a conspiracy theorist. She believes Trump is a saviour who activated Operation Warp Speed (a real government initiative to accelerate vaccine manufacture and distribution), while in the same breath decrying vaccines as dangerous substances and part of a long-standing global conspiracy to harm people. She is well-versed in the QAnon framework of interpreting drops and posts, analysing 'breadcrumbs' and finding hidden symbolism everywhere. She calls herself a 'digital soldier' who has a sacred mission to 'bring truth and light to the world'.

Kylie credits her moment of awakening, or 'red pill moment', to 2016, when she discovered the Australian Vaccination-risk Network, or AVN, and their spokesperson Meryl Dorey, whom she calls a 'hero'. She says this discovery triggered a memory of being deathly ill after a vaccination as a child, an incident that she claims her parents covered up, and she has been following the AVN's work ever since. Through the AVN she has discovered 'millions of other people' with similar stories.

As Kylie fell deeper into being a 'digital soldier', she would constantly post anti-vaccine and conspiracy content, which got her permanently banned from Facebook and Twitter. But she sees this as a validation of her truth and brushes it off, given how easy it is to move onto other platforms. 'I still have a YouTube channel, I'm on Instagram, and of course Telegram – Telegram is the best,' she explains.

Surprisingly, I find myself agreeing with Kylie's views on social media platforms. She declares that these platforms are a form of 'social engineering', trapping people into algorithmically curated tunnels and forcing them into hostile environments designed to trigger them into angry and divisive arguments. They are generally not good places for community and resolution, she believes. 'They want us to fight, they want us to hate one another, because divided, we're weaker.'

Her involvement in conspiracies had gradually alienated her from her 'old' friends and from family. At her lowest ebb, during a time she was most vulnerable and most isolated, when she had nothing to lose, she found promotions for the convoy to Canberra online. 'I literally just packed up the car, took my dog, and just went … I didn't know anyone who would be there.' But she felt that she was going to meet like-minded people, other 'light warriors' who shared her sacred mission of 'spreading truth to the world'. There she encountered 'millions' (the more accurate figure is hundreds) of other 'digital warriors, truthers, light bringers and sovereign citizens' wanting to expose the government and our health institutions. 'All these people, they've just had enough: enough of lockdowns, enough of the pandemic, enough of vaccines, enough of being told what to do.'

Now, she credits the convoy to Canberra as a source of new friends, new networks and a renewed sense of her mission. 'This is my tribe now, and there's so many of us all around the world,' she exclaims.

'Could they help you out of your current situation?' I ask. (She is still without an income and crashing on couches.)

She falls silent.

———————

Ash Jackson is living proof that there is a way out of the 'freedom' movement. But it took an accidental, catalytic moment for her to begin questioning its legitimacy. Like Kylie, and thousands of other Australians, she lost her job when Covid-19 hit and found herself isolated, helpless and alone. A musician by trade, her gigs dried up during the first wave, and she had nothing but time on her hands in her small Melbourne apartment when she started her journey down an online rabbit hole.

For Ash, it was less about QAnon or conspiracies and more about the idea that Australia was starting to become a police state, with authoritarian, brutal controls and law enforcement ensuring compliance above all else. She felt disgust at the arrest of Zoe Buhler, who tried to organise a small protest over Facebook and was filmed being handcuffed by police in her home. Buhler, twenty-eight, was pregnant at the time and unaware of the repercussions of organising a protest. 'I didn't realise that I wasn't allowed to,' she said. 'The police could have given me a phone call ...' Videos like these worked their way into Ash's feeds daily, until social media fed her mostly a diet of videos of police brutality and heavy-handed arrests. Eventually they led her to the social profiles of Reignite Democracy Australia. Monica Smit, Reignite Democracy's leader, welcomed Ash to the community, making her feel valued.

Ash's first anti-lockdown protest was an intoxicating experience. 'The atmosphere was amazing,' Ash recalls. 'It was like being at a rock concert and I was instantly welcomed by the rock stars … it felt incredible.'

This sense of solidarity is a common theme among freedom fighters. Having been ostracised by their existing networks for their beliefs (or even just emerging doubts) and so not being able to share them with anyone in their lives, the revelation of finding a group that accepted all they had to say 'felt like coming home'.

Ash, normally shy and reserved, found that she wanted more than anything to be a useful member of this new community. She was one of the earlier participants of the movement, 'when it was only a few hundred people', and became known to the inner circle. She threw herself into the organisation's activities, becoming a visible presence at demonstrations and even getting arrested several times. She describes vaguely 'some real full-on, illegal shit' that she was involved in planning, which she now deeply regrets.

For Ash, the turning point came during a protest in May 2021, by which time police had a good handle on the anti-vax movements and planning of demonstrations. After being asked by police to move on from the protest – they let her off with a warning – Ash instead went to a different area. There she found familiar faces in the crowd, including one of the leaders, Matt Lawson. 'Encouraged by other protestors to throw herself in front of police after receiving a move-on notice', as one media outlet noted, she led a charge, storming into an area filled with police. As she got closer, she looked back and realised she was alone.

Ash saw her comrades-in-arms sprinting away down the road. It was in this moment that the narratives around solidarity, community and 'where we go one, we go all' disintegrated.[5]

Deflated, Ash cooperated peacefully with the police, who simply asked her to go home. This was the beginning of her newfound respect for the police, who showed her civility, even though all she'd done in recent times was abuse them. Her respect was reinforced a few weeks later, when the police visited her home and she was arrested and taken in for questioning over certain activities, and the arresting officers were nothing but courteous. After her formal questioning, she got to know some of them, as she opened up about her struggles during the pandemic and began to connect with them. No charges were laid and Ash was even offered a lift home, 'a chat if you ever need it' and counselling services. Ash could no longer accept the idea of the police as brutal authoritarian monsters, which had got her into the 'freedom' movement in the first place.

Now, Ash has completely left the movement. 'I've deleted everything, unsubscribed from everyone,' she tells me, and she shares her story in the hope that others like her might find the inspiration to challenge the 'brainwashing'. She is also highly critical of the 'scam' aspects of the movement – when leaders raise funds for legal defences, campaigns and bail. 'Getting arrested was actually a good thing [for them], as this gives them the reason to fundraise and ask money from the community,' she says.

When I asked her what could have helped her leave the movement sooner, or what might have prompted her to question it earlier, she says, 'I don't know the answer to that. I feel very lucky that events happened for me the way they did, and hopefully my story might do that for someone else.'

It's important that we differentiate people like Scott, Kylie and Ash from other 'freedom fighter' bad actors who deliberately exploit others' anger, incite unrest and organise protests. Melbourne man Harrison McLean was one of the ringleaders behind several of the city's anti-lockdown protests. McLean organised protests through a network of private social media groups, including on Telegram and Gab, and expressed extreme far-right views in many of them, including antisemitism and racial hatred. *The Guardian* exposed his desire to spread disinformation: "'We start at 'Dan Bad' and go right through to 'No Coercive Vaccines' and get into the Pedo suppression orders and NWO agenda and One world government as a concept to be opposed," he wrote, echoing a laundry list of baseless and antisemitic conspiracy theories that have found a fresh audience during the pandemic.'[6] He was charged with incitement in September 2021.

Monica Smit, founder and (according to her LinkedIn profile) managing director of Reignite Democracy Australia, is one of the better-known 'freedom' movement and anti-lockdown organisers. She has even been mentioned on US far-right conspiracy theory websites such as Alex Jones's InfoWars, along with her fiancé, Morgan C. Jonas. The former reality television wannabe – her *Survivor* audition tape is on YouTube – was arrested and charged with incitement in September 2021 in relation to two protests. One of these, held on 21 August, was described by Victoria Police's Chief Commissioner Shane Patton as 'probably one of the most violent protests we've seen in nearly 20 years', as police were hit with projectiles, punched and kicked by members of the thousands-strong crowd.[7]

Christian 'Mack' Marchegiani is considered a powerful voice for the 'freedom' movement and, despite being described by *The Sydney*

Morning Herald as a 'conspiracy theorist', his content gets shared regularly. He is one of the co-founders of 'Reclaim the Line', a group that is anti–vaccine mandates (their website is emblazoned with the line 'The brave may not live forever, but the captive do not live at all'), and was a key voice encouraging people to participate in the convoy to Canberra.[8] In September 2022, he launched an online petition and promised a rally 'in every capital city of Australia' to 'demand justice for the Australian people' and 'hold the government and police to account for their abuse of powers'.[9]

McLean, Smit, Marchegiani and their ilk promote themselves actively through online channels and regularly fundraise for their causes, with their unquestioning followers seemingly happy to oblige.

The commercial aspect to the 'freedom fighter' movement has similarities with that of the sophisticated network of MAGA advocates in the United States, who spruik merchandise online and call on their support base for donations. Reignite Democracy Australia sells caps, T-shirts and bumper stickers, and raises money for media campaigns and legal battles. The Australian Vaccination-risk Network, which has been described as 'Australia's most active counter-vaccine lobby group', sells DVDs and books alongside membership subscriptions in their online shop. They use the profits to amplify their anti-vaccination and anti-science messages, even though the vast majority of doctors and reams of scientific evidence have long supported – and continue to support – the view that vaccination is safe.[10]

There is little question for me that groups such as these are spreading disinformation. I cannot hold any sympathy for these groups or their leaders. Those who orchestrate and promote 'freedom' movement protests and anti-vaccination messages, and profit off others' participation, need to be held to account, legally and morally, by all of us.

The psychology of vaccine hesitancy

Unsurprisingly, protests, riots and civil unrest are known to occur during times of great upheaval and uncertainty, such as plagues and pandemics. Throughout history, there have been clashes between the authorities and those who believed those authorities were trying to cause them harm, rather than help. As far back as the fourteenth century, fights broke out in Venice during the bubonic plague over scant resources and mass unemployment. During the late nineteenth century, mobs rioted in Wisconsin during a smallpox outbreak, fearful that the authorities were hiding the sick and misrepresenting the true extent of the epidemic. Amid the 1968 Hong Kong flu, panic buying of medication led to shortages that caused riots and looting.[11] In a 2013 SARS outbreak, frightened Chinese villagers stormed a local government office where patients were being quarantined. In 2014, health workers were murdered by villagers in Guinea, West Africa, who feared that they were spreading Ebola.

Protests, riots and civil unrest are more likely to occur when groups form grievances against those in positions of authority, whom they come to distrust and blame, or who may have imposed restrictions these groups feel are too harsh or unwarranted. A couple of key themes influenced those who were most likely to protest the pandemic lockdowns and restrictions: a belief in conspiracy theories around the pandemic made adherents feel the public health restrictions were a form of unwarranted control or part of a wider government 'plot', and a scepticism of vaccinations led to a conviction that mandates were an imposition.

In Chapter 1 we saw how QAnon enables widespread conspiratorial thinking and how the movement grew to accommodate other conspiracy theories. During the pandemic, some in the wellness movement who were vaccine sceptics found their way into QAnon, which amalgamated many of their anti-science, anti-institutional ideas into an overall conspiracy narrative involving the harmful effects of vaccinations and the abuse of government control. Some protested against lockdowns and public health mandates – a smaller number are still protesting today.

In 2019, the World Health Organization declared vaccine hesitancy one of the top global health threats. The WHO's statement was unambiguous: vaccine hesitancy 'threatens to reverse progress made in tackling vaccine-preventable diseases', jeopardising the millions of lives saved by vaccination.[12] Research suggests that vaccine hesitancy has increased in recent years, including among unlikely candidates such as healthcare workers. A study conducted at the University of Kent in Canterbury, England, found that exposure to anti-vaccine conspiracy theories significantly negatively influenced vaccine intentions. Conspiracy theories 'appear to introduce undue suspicion about vaccine safety, and increase feelings of powerlessness and disillusionment, whilst decreasing trust in authorities, which in turn introduce reluctance to vaccinate', the authors wrote.[13]

One of the main reasons for vaccine hesitancy is psychological reactance. A team of scientists led by Christina Steindl paraphrase US psychologists Jack and Sharon Brehm, describing psychological reactance as 'an unpleasant motivational arousal that emerges when people experience a threat to or loss of their free behaviours. It serves as a motivator to restore one's freedom … In general, people are convinced that they possess certain freedoms to engage in so-called free behaviours. Yet there are times when they cannot, at least feel that they cannot, do so.'[14] Brehm gives examples of being forced to pay fees, being prohibited from using a phone in certain settings, or being instructed to do something by your boss that you don't want to.

Psychologist Steven Taylor elaborates, saying that attempts at persuading reactants to accept a particular view 'may paradoxically strengthen their beliefs against that view': 'A person might endorse anti-science beliefs in an attempt to establish their self-image as a nonconformist … thus, a message that threatens that person's freedom – such as a health warning to get immunized – can induce psychological reactance, which in turn can motivate the person to restore freedom by such means as derogating the source or by adopting a position that is opposite of that advocated.'[15]

A University of Sydney study found that people in several countries, including Australia, the United States, the United Kingdom and Canada, who deliberately breach pandemic-related health restrictions shared certain characteristics. Around 10 per cent of the population were found to be noncompliant towards Covid-19 restrictions. These people were mostly men, were inclined to be less cooperative and less considerate, and were overall less intellectual, less willing to try new experiences and more extroverted. They tended to be older than youths, to prioritise their own interests and to place a high value on 'freedom'. They also believed their social culture to be tolerant of a degree of deviant behaviour. These individuals were less likely to engage with government announcements and had unhealthy coping techniques, such as substance abuse.[16]

The convoy to Canberra also represented a deep sense of disenfranchisement among those who felt they had been pushed to the brink by lockdowns and vaccination mandates. Kylie, and many like her, were buoyed by the sense of community and solidarity that permeated the convoy. People coming together en masse, uniting for a common cause, sharing grievances, validating each other's beliefs without a sense of being ridiculed and dismissed – it all felt like a salve to the trauma of the pandemic. While some in attendance clearly had dangerous intentions, there were many looking for recognition, for legitimacy, to be heard or to rail against the powerful institutions they felt had long been ignoring them.

It would be foolish to ignore the degree of sentiment that events like the convoy gave rise to for some of the participants, and it would compound their trauma to dismiss them uniformly as loonies. Part of the attraction of the 'freedom' movement is this sense of social connection, and we need to address this reality if we are to reach some of these people.

Bad ideas go viral

Many extremist groups gather online to organise their activities. In the lead-up to the anti-lockdown protests, hundreds of far-right groups took to Facebook to discuss tactical strategies, combat medicine and weaponry, including how to create explosives and use flame throwers.

In the United States, the 'boogaloo' movement is a collection of loosely aligned far-right groups who believe in a pending civil war: the 'boogaloo'. In 2019 and 2020, members of these groups, often called 'boogaloo boys', shared detailed tactics and promoted violence against the authorities for several months with no intervention from Facebook. When Facebook announced in July 2020 that it was banning these violent groups, many thought action came too late. *The Guardian* noted, 'This anti-government "boogaloo" rhetoric has already been publicly linked to at least 15 arrests and five deaths, including the murder of a federal security guard and a sheriff's deputy in California, according to media reports and analysts who track extremists.'[17] It is difficult to avoid the conclusion that Facebook only leapt into action once the presence of these groups on their platform generated mainstream media coverage, and even then some believe the company's intervention was ad-hoc and ineffective.

The most popular boogaloo-themed pages on Facebook attracted more than 30,000 followers at their peak. The pages generated income from selling merchandise and clothing. The administrators were organised and had various other private groups, including those that focused on intelligence gathering, technology, communication, machinery, combat medicine and weaponry. The groups have ties to white supremacist movements and regularly praise Hitler and promote white supremacist ideologies. Boogaloo members exchange military materials, planning documents and CIA handbooks using open-source intelligence. They share instructions for how to make bombs. The groups encourage violence and targeted assaults on specific figures.[18]

In Australia, a German-based conspiracy group called Worldwide Demonstration helped to coordinate several protests through Telegram, Instagram and Facebook. Their messages were regularly promoted by popular anti-vax and conspiracy pages and influencers. Astonishingly, the group was able to publicise protests in places as far from Germany as Townsville, Cairns, Darwin and Hobart.[19] Local organisers adapted the global campaign and shared it across their pages under the title 'Australia Freedom Rally'. Another organiser, 'Australians vs The Agenda', coordinated protests using their Telegram and Instagram accounts, reaching more than 30,000 followers. Individual groups shared vast numbers of conspiracy theories, ranging from climate denial to vaccine safety issues, QAnon and antisemitic content. Local 'influencers' helped to amplify events on social media and draw crowds.

One of these was 24-year-old Jon-Bernard Kairouz – who rose to have his five minutes of fame by 'predicting' local New South Wales Covid-19 case numbers on TikTok. A vocal attendee at the protest, he addressed the crowd through a megaphone, touting himself as 'the people's premier' and saying that it was 'time for freedom'. (Two months later, he was in hospital with Covid-19.)[20]

Tim Watts, then Shadow Assistant Minister for Communications and Cybersecurity, remarked that largely fringe groups with fringe views could, through social media, give the appearance of having wide traction and a large support base. 'These are minority, marginal views. A very tiny proportion of the population share these views but unfortunately the views of these people are amplified by social media platforms, and they're more easily able to find other people with their stupid and selfish views on social media platforms, and they're able to organise to the detriment of the entire country,' said Watts.[21]

Even 'casual' observers like Scott, whom we met earlier, calls out social media for amplifying the intensity and divisiveness of these alternative viewpoints, as platforms send the user down rabbit holes that overwhelm and often radicalise, given the sheer magnitude of content from around the world.

Canada's 'Freedom convoy' inspired copycat groups and channels across Facebook, Instagram and Telegram. Facebook and Instagram – despite many, many announcements of crackdowns against illegal and harmful groups – continue to host active groups and content associated with the convoys. On Instagram, attendees use live-streaming, 'stories', videos and images to praise themselves and spread the message globally. Many groups that are being monitored by Facebook's AI have learned to change names and titles, simply swapping out terms such as 'anti-vaccination' and 'Trump' for 'freedom', 'trucker' and 'convoy'. This is a twisted mix of self-manifestation and wish fulfilment, given their common belief about coded language and secret messages everywhere. There is also evidence of foreign content farms in Bangladesh, Vietnam and Romania capitalising on the chaos of the pandemic and developing groups and content to promote the convoys. They have similarly switched from banned conspiracy themes and content to trucker-related content.

Australia's convoy to Canberra, a collection of disparate groups – including sovereign citizens, ultraconservative Christians, conspiracy theorists and anti-vaxxers – were all brought together by one common force: social media. Many are unaware of the extent to which overseas groups with vastly different motives, as well as coordinated overseas content farms, were the real drivers of their local 'sacred movement'. These groups can ultimately be linked back to Trump's brand of fake news–inspired campaigning and social chaos, which uses online platforms as a weapon to mobilise people to anger. The very same people pop up again and again running these sorts of groups – they simply change their names and details each time one group is banned and launch another.

One of Trump's most devastating legacies is the establishment of this type of network of disinformation: fuelled and amplified by social networks, using overseas content farms that capitalise on unregulated online platforms, amplified and abused by bad actors and public figures who profit from these groups, and with a technological architecture which feeds on the anger and frustration of some of our most vulnerable citizens. Almost six years after Trump came to power, the same large online platforms – Facebook, Instagram, YouTube and Twitter – continue to be used to spread chaos and disinformation, recruiting freedom fighters all over the world.

Who has the right to protest and where?

The right to protest is critical in a democracy. We should be able to question government policy, corporate policy or any initiative significant enough that it affects the community at large. Freedom of speech is, after all, a human right, according to the United Nations' Universal Declaration.

This has been a key argument used by freedom fighters. While Australians do not have a constitutional right to freedom of speech, as in America, we do have the United Nations–enshrined rights 'to freedom of opinion and expression' and 'freedom of peaceful assembly and association', which extends to public protest. What many freedom fighters fail to realise is that these rights are not absolute. A government can place limits on freedom of expression and freedom of assembly when the exercise of those rights stands to cause harm to the rest of society – namely, in matters of national security, public order and public health.

By defying public health orders to gather (typically mask-less) at rallies, freedom fighters put themselves and others at risk of contracting Covid-19. The violent protests at Melbourne at the CFMMEU building gave rise to a cluster of infections and fears of a superspreader event. Protests in Sydney led to similar concerns. Police, journalists and frontline healthcare workers all had their safety put at risk. The protests became a tyranny of the minority as a small group of anti-vaccination and anti-lockdown supporters held public streets to siege and generated anxiety, fear and concern among many in the community – all to exercise their rights to expression and assembly.

There are ways to conduct protests in virtual spaces. Climate activist Greta Thunberg had recommended online protests during risky pandemic settings. Others have suggested physical protests that comply with public health orders around social distancing and mask wearing. So freedom fighters could in fact exercise their right to assembly even in a pandemic context. But that wouldn't have the same headline-grabbing effect, would it?

Breaking free of freedom fighters

Social media has helped people gather and build momentum around worthy issues. Think of how Greta Thunberg's lone climate protest outside the Swedish parliament in 2018 was shared widely on Facebook and YouTube, sparking a global movement, or how the revolutionary wave of demonstrations against corruption that became the Arab Spring was amplified by Twitter. The Black Lives Matter movement, highlighting racial injustice and systemic inequality, began in the United States but was soon taken up globally via the internet, including by Indigenous Australians. Marriage equality campaigners across Australia used online channels to great effect to demand equal rights to marriage for queer people, enlivened by changes to legislation overseas. The hashtag #ChangetheDate gets traction every January as more Australians each year protest the nation celebrating Australia Day on 26 January.

But while online platforms can facilitate the exercise of our democratic rights for worthwhile causes, they can also do so for less enlightened causes. Most freedom fighters found their way into the movement online. Many technology companies claim to be 'neutral' – that is, they provide a platform but are not responsible for, and do not promote, the content that appears on this platform. Yet where but on these platforms could a would-be freedom fighter encounter such a wealth of misinformation and disinformation; algorithms that promote sensationalism, anger and outrage; and content peddled by miscreants? It stands to reason that this environment could facilitate views that are more harmful than not.

Freedom fighters are a direct result of the uncertainty and challenge of the pandemic. This period of social chaos was ripe for conspiracy theorists and bad actors to mutate and multiply: to make their conspiracies more elaborate and increase their follower base. Many freedom fighters are also online conspiracy theorists, and the interventions for online conspiracy theorists in Chapter 1 may also apply.

However, not all freedom fighters are in the grips of conspiracy. Some are disenfranchised in other ways. Many experienced real trauma during the pandemic, including losing their jobs, homes and loved ones. The unfortunate reality is that we will not know the full picture of the trauma induced by the pandemic for many years, as we continue to live with the virus and its impacts. Australia's experience of pandemic has also been compounded by recent natural disasters such as floods and the Black Summer bushfires, and by geopolitical instability over China – not to mention the Russian invasion of Ukraine, which has sent shockwaves across the entire world. We are living through a time of grief and loss, and many are trying to process this in varied ways. The freedom fighter is one manifestation of this. With this in mind, the interventions recommended for the freedom fighter focus on support for these people during the pandemic and its aftermath.

What can individuals do?

Stay connected to others in their lives

Many Australians have never had significant restrictions imposed on their freedoms before, and the experience of state-driven rules was an unwelcome novelty. Some have enjoyed relative prosperity, and they struggled during lockdowns when forced to curtail their usual hobbies, travel plans and social outings. Others saw the pandemic push them lower on the socio-economic ladder, as they lost jobs and housing.

While we hope that lockdowns are behind us, the uncertainty is not. Maintaining a sense of equilibrium in the face of the unknown is something we can all strive for. This might mean trying not to plan too far into the future or to manage situations with uncontrollable features but focusing on daily tasks and celebrating getting through these. Actively working on building resilience could help alleviate some feelings of anxiety and hopelessness and leave us better equipped to confront problems when they do materialise.

There are a range of support services that offer resources and counselling centred on Covid-19 and the effects of the pandemic. Organisations such as Beyond Blue, Lifeline, the Black Dog Institute, ReachOut, Head to Health and headspace provide support for those who need a mental health partner. Details are listed in the 'Resources' section at the end of this book. There are some common themes and recommendations across these groups, including:

- Staying connected with friends and family, ideally through video and phone calls, to keep up meaningful relationships.
- Planning enjoyable activities, including making time to be active, eat well and relax.
- Managing the consumption of information – including controlling consumption of media – if it is causing stress and anxiety. We all need a break from our news feeds sometimes.
- Making realistic plans to help maintain a sense of control and agency, whether it's a to-do list to lessen overwhelm, a budgeting spreadsheet or a mental health plan developed with a health practitioner.

Share credible information

Much like conspiracy theorists, freedom fighters often reject facts, particularly around the topics of health and vaccination. Studies or figures on, say, the safety of vaccines may be dismissed in favour of anecdote. But unlike conspiracy theorists, who may feel their beliefs have a hold over them, many freedom fighters may marshal incorrect information as a form of justification for their actions. They are only acting against perceived injustices or impositions on their rights or freedoms, they may say.

This is a tricky dynamic to detangle. But often what lies at the root of this insistence on 'freedom' is a sense of uncertainty and fear. Rather than getting caught in a conversation about which rights trump which, any person trying to reach a freedom fighter or wanting to leave that world themselves should share credible facts, well-reasoned research and public health advice on a regular basis. Making sure that any information is from authoritative sources – including the World Health Organization, public health departments and established scientific and medical professionals – will help to combat the power of inaccurate information or hearsay.

Disconnect from sites that promote anger and violence

Many freedom fighters believe that they are victims. It seems to them as though the authorities impose public health orders and mandates without considering how it affects their lives and livelihoods. This can lead to a sense of discontent and frustration, until the only logical response seems to be to 'fight back'. Online 'freedom' groups, some of which have alt-right connections, stoke individuals' discontent into a white-hot anger. They may have agendas that have little to do with vaccination or mandates, and more to do with fomenting chaos and violence, even bringing down the government. Disengaging from such websites, social media pages and influencers and the toxic messages they present may result in a healthier overall attitude towards the pandemic and its impact.

Encourage supportive offline friends and networks

One of the key drivers of freedom fighters is that they feel ostracised for their beliefs. Through online platforms, they have found others who are feeling the same way. This sense of solidarity reinforces their beliefs and can create an us-versus-them mentality where they feel they are lone crusaders in an indifferent world.

One of the many downsides of the internet is that it increases polarisation and tribalism by facilitating niche groups. The online world does not foster an environment where disagreements or differences can be explored civilly and respectfully. It's important, therefore, that those trying to reach freedom fighters emphasise the value of real-world networks versus the online counterparts. Avoid being hostile towards someone's beliefs or mocking them, and instead come from a place of compassion. Listen to their experiences and focus on things that are you have in common, which transcend the pandemic – shared histories, localities, habits or likes, and mutual friends. Only by maintaining a genuine relationship with them can you hope to influence unhealthy behaviour and attitudes.

What can governments and society do?

Strong public health policy and support

While there may always be those who are opposed to government and its institutions, during times of crisis it is precisely government's job to step in and develop public health policy to protect the community. As we've seen around the world during the pandemic, the most effective government responses were measured, were based on public health advice and placed the community's safety at the centre of decision-making. Policies that have overtly favoured commercial outcomes or are based on abstract views around supporting 'the economy' – divorced from the people who participate in that economy – have usually proven to be disastrous for the community at large.

During times of uncertainty and trouble, governments need to develop adequate support programs to help people get through. The Australian federal government's JobKeeper package was one such important support, which kept many from slipping into poverty. Others who were affected by the pandemic did not receive the support they needed, like Kylie, who was rendered jobless and homeless but, she says, she she was still not able to access government assistance.

On other levels, the government response has been an abject failure. The Australian government did not purchase enough vaccines early enough, the vaccine rollout was inefficient and the messaging attached to it was often confusing. Many felt unprepared for changes and unsupported as they navigated them. The lack of a concerted public awareness campaign that informed and incentivised people to get vaccinated, and provided the right levels of support to do so, no doubt led to many feeling disenfranchised and may have pushed some towards becoming freedom fighters. Ultimately, the government's failure to manage the pandemic with strong community support services during the vaccine rollout was a factor in the formation of an angry, confused, sometimes desperate mob who felt compelled to drive all the way to Canberra to register their protest.

Dedicated mental health support services during crises

Psychologist Steven Taylor, who specialises in anxiety disorders and has written a book about psychological responses to pandemics, has argued for greater mental health support during pandemics. He describes how the lack of mental health support systems can increase the risk that people will develop emotional and psychological disorders during these periods.

Taylor advocates the 'screen-and-treat' approach. An example of a successful screen-and-treat approach to mental health support occurred following the 2005 terrorist bombings in London. Mental health support was promoted to health workers and the public, creating broad awareness. A dedicated 24-hour hotline was established to provide general mental health advice. This hotline also acted as a triage service. Client cases were trafficked based on their urgency: for example, they might be referred to psychologists, referred to doctors for immediate treatment or referred to counselling services for further monitoring. The hotline provided a means to identify those who would benefit from early intervention, preventing the development of more serious or persistent disorders later. The government acknowledged the mental health burden of disasters and created treatment programs specifically to address the psychic wounds, not only the physical injuries. This approach also limited the burden on health workers who may not have had the training to treat mental health issues yet encountered them daily in a general population suffering from trauma and distress.

In the context of a pandemic or another community crisis that warrants a public health response, a treat-and-screen approach could provide much-needed support and assistance to those who may be at risk of becoming freedom fighters due to the mental health burden. Simply having access to a mental health professional to discuss their anxieties and frustrations with, and be listened to in a sincere, objective and professional manner, might reduce the chance that they will slip into social isolation and mental anguish. This approach could thus create overall public health benefits by limiting the number of people who may want to breach public health orders.

Access to credible, evidence-based information

'The truth is paywalled but the lies are free,' journalist Nathan J. Robinson wrote in *Current Affairs* magazine in August 2020. This is an apt description of our information ecosystem, where authoritative journalism, news and scientific research are often behind paywalls, or are more difficult to access than misinformation, anecdote and hearsay, which runs rampant on social media platforms and the internet more broadly.

The battleground for truth and accurate information grows daily as keyboard warriors and self-publishers of all sorts spread falsehoods with little consequence. We must once again establish a culture and a public square based on facts and worthwhile discussion. This involves strengthening the infrastructure around news and communication, like investing in public interest journalism and public broadcasters – whose missions are to communicate facts, inform and educate for the public benefit. This could also mean a reimagining of the spaces which now serve as our public town halls – which are private and for-profit digital platforms that are not suited to this purpose.

Penalties and bans for bad actors

The ringleaders who incite, organise and mobilise against health mandates bear much of the blame for the phenomenon of the freedom fighter. For all the thousands of people who have been duped or radicalised into accepting freedom fighter ideologies, there are a handful who are deliberately fostering, manufacturing and capitalising on this dissent.

A report by the UK non-profit Centre for Countering Digital Hate found that twelve people were behind most of the disinformation and lies about Covid-19 vaccines shared on social media. Dubbed the 'Disinformation Dozen', this group was responsible for 65 per cent of shares of anti-vaccine misinformation on social media platforms.[22] Such individuals profit from disinformation, amassing millions of followers and selling them questionable supplements and resources. Facebook only took down these accounts after the report publicly exposed them. In Australia, a similar pattern is evident, with a small group of 'influencers' responsible for the most dangerous misinformation about the Covid-19 vaccine. Some of these have been banned from social media platforms after they made media headlines, but others continue to peddle their dangerous content today.

Similarly, groups and influencers from other countries can use social media to create a network of followers, giving the illusion of legitimacy and a groundswell of public support. These freedom fighter ringleaders and disinformation superspreaders are deliberately polluting our information ecosystem with lies and falsehoods, spreading confusion and harming the public, including those who are vulnerable to alternative ideas. They must be weeded out and penalised.

Regulations on the platforms that support bad actors

While freedom fighters will continue to exist without online platforms, these platforms have allowed peddlers of disinformation to communicate their ideas to a mainstream audience, provided a digital space for them to gather supporters en masse, and facilitated the coordination and promotion of content through their networks. The business models of Facebook and YouTube foster the kind of hysterical, polarised, hyperpartisan divides that encourage freedom fighters and their way of thinking.

Years of self-regulation by Facebook and YouTube have barely had any effect on the problem, while the number of people exposed to disinformation is increasing daily. These online platforms must be held to account for the content being posted and real-world illegal action being discussed on their channels. Only strong regulations and material penalties will force these companies to take serious action to address the harms being done by their products.

Currently Australia's only answer to disinformation and misinformation is a paltry voluntary code with no material fines and no independent oversight. This is not enough in an environment where Australians can encounter misinformation daily. We must develop strong regulations around misinformation and online safety to address the toxic business model of Big Tech platforms and protect ourselves and our loved ones.

———

If we are to negotiate the challenges that Big Tech poses, we must come together as groups, communities and societies to confront them. We cannot enable a world of division and chaos – the Freedom Fighter is just one example of what this leads to.

We must also ensure that we do not ignore those most vulnerable. Only a society that prioritises equality truly guarantees us freedom from the Freedom Fighter.

3

The Social Media Narcissist

In the future, everything will be live-streamed. We'll all be wearing camera-enabled devices that track, record and broadcast our every move, thought and action. We'll tune into one another's streams and gain an intimate knowledge of each other's everyday lives. Nothing will be secret – everything will be 'transparent'.

American author David Eggers posited this as a nightmarish scenario in his 2013 novel *The Circle*. A young, ambitious employee of an omnipotent technology company modelled on Google agrees to be the first person to go 'fully transparent', whereby she straps a camera to her person and live-streams everything she does, sees and encounters daily, becoming an online sensation. This gross abuse of privacy is exemplified in a scene where the protagonist visits her ageing parents and accidentally walks in on them being intimate, broadcasting their private moment to the world.

Eggers meant for this to be a cautionary tale. But less than a decade later, it comes close to describing our reality, where most of us carry smartphones that can capture and record our every move, and many of us broadcast our lives and daily activities through our social media feeds. The pathological need to share is on display in the TikTok streams of millions of teens and tweens; Instagram feeds from wellness practitioners, 'mummy bloggers' and aspiring models; and Twitter thought bubbles from our politicians and public figures.

The selfie perhaps encapsulates this phenomenon best. In 2013, 'selfie' was added to the *Oxford English Dictionary* and subsequently celebrated as one of the 'words of the year'. Usage of the word had jumped 17,000 per cent from the year before. The *OED* defined a selfie as 'a photograph that one has taken of oneself, typically with a smartphone or webcam and uploaded to a social media website'. We love taking selfies and do it everywhere: at home, at work, at the beach, at events, on holidays. We take selfies during mundane, daily activities like cooking and walking the dog, and during momentous occasions, such as anniversaries, weddings and graduations. Selfies reveal our desire to be seen, to capture our experiences and say: *I am here. Please look at me.*

Some even put their lives in danger to take a good selfie. In 2015, two Russian men in the Ural mountains died after posing with a hand grenade with the pin pulled out. Dozens of selfie-related deaths that year led to the Russian Interior Ministry launching a 'safe selfie' guide. At Xixiajou Wildlife Park in China, a tourist was reportedly dragged underwater and killed by a walrus after trying to take a selfie with it and losing his footing, slipping into the walrus's pool. At Yellowstone National Park in the United States, Reuters reported that 'exasperated officials issued warnings after five separate selfie takers were gored this summer while standing too near bison'. Turkish researchers found that the most common examples of selfie-related deaths include drowning, falling, getting crushed by trains, gunshots and electrocutions.

Jesse Fox, assistant professor of communications at Ohio State University, says that selfies attract risk-takers and those in search of attention. 'It's all about me. It's putting me in the frame. I'm getting attention and when I post that to social media, I'm getting the confirmation that I need from other people that I'm awesome.'[1]

It's not just ourselves we endanger, either. In 2017, British multimedia artist Simon Birch held an immersive exhibition at the 14th Factory pop-up gallery in Los Angeles. One installation housed a series of pedestals, each featuring a crown. It was a beautiful piece, exceptionally selfie-worthy. An overenthusiastic selfie-taker got too close to the work and sent the pedestals toppling, domino-style, across the gallery, causing around US$200,000 in damages.[2]

We also harm the natural world with our selfie-taking – national parks, fragile trees and even wildlife. In the Amazon, the mighty anaconda has been reduced to a tourist prop. Large snakes are kept in cramped, dark wooden crates in cities such as Manaus, Brazil, and Puerto Alegria, Peru, dehydrated and hot while waiting for the next tourist selfie opportunity.

So why are we so compelled to keep taking selfies?

Selfies as performance

Selfies are an expression of our pervasive desire to present ourselves to the world in a certain way. But this desire has a longer history. In 1959, sociologist Erving Goffman published what would become a key text in the field, *The Presentation of Self in Everyday Life*. The book studies how people display different versions of themselves in different parts of their lives – at work, at home and in public. Goffman likened this to a performance, each of us successfully 'staging' a character in each of these situations.[3] Most of us can relate to this idea of versions of self as we think about how we navigate our different circles and experiences.

In 1950's *The Lonely Crowd*, sociologist David Riesman (in collaboration with colleagues Reuel Denney and Nathan Glazer) wrote about how post–World War II American society turned from an 'inner to an other directed sense of self'.[4] Individuals shifted from an inner-facing identity to projecting their identities outwards in an effort to seek social approval. In modern suburban 'tribes', white middle-class Americans strove for conformity: 'Without a firm sense of purpose, people looked to their neighbours for validation.' Riesman was one of the first commentators on the rise of consumer culture and predicted how we would use consumer goods and products as expressions of our identities: *I am wealthy if I have this household appliance; I am feminine if I have this item of clothing; I am manly if I buy this brand of aftershave.* The 'other-directed' identity looked to their neighbours, peers and media personalities for cues on what to consume, how to behave and how to 'be'.

American theorist Judith Butler goes one step further and claims that identity is retroactively created by our performance of self. Twentieth-century French philosopher Maurice Merleau-Ponty suggested that we create and develop our identities 'through an active process of embodying certain cultural and historical possibilities'. He meant that we are all products of our times, and we embody certain values and standards and 'perform' in a certain way based on the beliefs held in our moment in history. Butler took Merleau-Ponty's concept and contemporised it, dubbing this 'performativity'. For Butler, the performance *is* identity, a 'lived experience' that we cultivate over time. Butler does not believe that we each have an 'inner' or 'unique' identity, but that our identities are developed through our activities, behaviours and gestures. For both Merleau-Ponty and Butler, identity is a social construct.[5]

We may not feel like it when we're posing in front of a bathroom mirror, angling our phone to find the best lighting, but our selfie-taking is part of a long tradition of presentation and performance. Following Goffman's 'versioning' and Butler's 'performativity', the selfie is an active, conscious construction of identity. It is our way of showing what we deem desirable – and our understanding of what is deemed desirable is shaped by our moment in history. When a guy on Instagram posts a gym selfie, surrounded by weights, flexing just so, he is telling the world that he is active, virile and fit – what he perceives as desirable traits for a young man. The selfie is not unlike a commissioned portrait in times past, where, say, a rich seventeenth-century Dutch merchant would be depicted in fine garments indicating wealth and alongside exotic objects symbolising travel and prestige. The difference is that, on the internet, a selfie is not designed to be viewed in isolation. Our construction of identity is a constant process, which continues after the initial post has been uploaded, and even while the subject is offline. Curated feeds and comments create a world in which performativity is heightened. The internet has provided a global audience for our neuroses, the smartphone an instantaneous recording and editing device for our images, and social media a network to validate, comment, inspire or judge.

Exposure or exposed?

Anne aspires to be the ultimate Insta-mum. She loves hosting birthday parties for her children, putting on lavish events in beautiful settings with stylish décor and magazine-worthy cakes and pastries. Before she became a full-time mum she was a graphic designer, so she has an innate sense of style and an appreciation for good visuals. These days she finds that Instagram can offer that same feeling of satisfaction she used to get from a job well done for a client. She is beginning to tag major brands (baby clothing stores, dessert companies, furniture retailers) in her posts to demonstrate how brand-friendly her content and her lifestyle is. By doing this she is hoping for a sponsorship deal or a brand partnership – a 'collab'.

Inside Anne's bright, spacious house on Sydney's North Shore on the day of her daughter's first birthday, the living room is decorated with tasteful birthday garlands and streamers. A side table already overflows with presents, at least a dozen or so, even though guests are only just arriving. The living and dining space open to a deck of varnished wood and a backyard ready to receive children, with toys and a colourful cubby house.

The kitchen has scenes ready for photographing. One corner has a row of tiny milk bottles that have been filled with either chocolate or vanilla milk, in an alternating pattern. These are lined up like soldiers to serve to the over-sugared toddlers running around once the photographs are complete. A coloured shelf holds a neat line-up of decorated take-home goodie bags for later.

On a table for adults – placed at a focal point in the kitchen so guests can admire the perfectly appointed display – sweet and savoury canapés are nestled among lively decorations. Two thickly frosted layer cakes, both a shade of creamy vanilla with unique but complementary decorations, are perched on trays.

The event begins as a pleasant suburban get-together. Outside, past the airy deck, parents try to chat while excited children run around in the yard and the hosts fuss over new arrivals. Someone is barbecuing. The setting could not be more idyllic and Australian.

All of a sudden, there is a professional photographer on the scene. I don't notice her until she starts elbowing her way in to take shots of the children and the guests talking, encouraging us to 'keep acting naturally'. We roll our eyes at one another and play along, chatting self-consciously as she snaps away. Thankfully, she soon moves on, directing Anne around, photographing her in different locations.

As Anne manoeuvres her sick one-year-old (she's been unwell all week) into a perfectly produced scene, ready for her Instagram moment, there are several painful minutes when her daughter wails in protest. Anne persists, against her child's banshee screams and thrashing arms, lining up with each family group to pose against her Insta-perfect backdrop. Her daughter won't stop crying the whole time. The photographer mutters something about editing the photos.

Oh well, kids will be kids, right?

A few days after the party, the official photographs are released on Instagram and Facebook – heavily edited and carefully selected shots. The comments are all gushing, attendees declaring they had 'the most wonderful time' (including the photographer, who was there for all of fifteen minutes).

It makes me uncomfortable. Anne spent all this time, effort and money on her event and she deserves to celebrate and create memories. As a friend, I support her in this. But I can't shake the feeling that for Anne, the party did not matter as much as its online representation. A get-together doesn't need the perfect decorations, catering and photographs to prove it a success. If I were being harsh, I might suggest that the event was an excuse for Anne, despite her sick child, to chase a picture-perfect vision she had for her Instagram feed. What she wanted was a film set, and the guests were the extras.

Was Anne putting her need for validation above all else that day? Well, parenting is difficult enough without others throwing rocks. No doubt we didn't see the days she spent nursing her daughter in the lead-up to the party. Undocumented are the weeks and months of pure child-rearing, emotional and exhausting.

But what compelled Anne to act this way on her child's birthday? And why were we all willingly complicit in her desire to enact a performative display just for the Insta bragging rights afterwards?

––––––––––

James is a self-declared 'social media influencer' who resides in Sydney's inner city but 'practically lives in the Eastern Suburbs'. He is in his twenties and works as a real estate agent, but his passion is fitness and fashion, and his social media presence, particularly his Instagram, is central to this. He is proud of his follower count (just over 150,000). 'It's gotten me sponsorships, brand ambassador offers, modelling contracts,' he boasts. 'It's also helped me launch my own fashion label online.'

James was originally from regional New South Wales but always had his sights set on the big city, in particular Sydney's larger gay scene. Now he feels central to and known within Sydney's gay community. 'People recognise me [from Instagram] … I usually get looks of recognition [when I go out].'

His Instagram profile consists almost entirely of 'thirst traps' – posts designed to generate attention with sexually charged images and videos. This is mainly photos of him posing shirtless, often in underwear. He is classically handsome and well built and is proud of his physique and his looks. When I ask him whether he feels the pressure to keep in shape, he laughs. 'It's what [my audience] wants – they follow me for my fitness photos and my lifestyle.'

'Lifestyle' in his case seems to involve being in Speedos in various Sydney hotspots, holding drinks in restaurants, bars and cafes, and standing in or beside the water in exotic locations. James started a limited series podcast with a collaborator to promote this lifestyle, extolling the virtues of his fabulous weekends and his social media presence. They abandoned it after a couple of episodes following some harsh online criticism. He chooses not to answer questions around 'that podcast' and says only that his Instagram profile continues to bring him success. 'People see me as someone to aspire to,' he says, without a hint of coyness. 'Social media provides me with a creative outlet and helps me express myself and showcase my habits.'

What is an 'influencer' anyway?

Influencers are personalities who have amassed followers on social media by posting regular content – in particular on Instagram, YouTube and TikTok, platforms that encourage and reward 'creator' output. Influencers are notably different from qualified professionals who happen to be influential on social platforms (including journalists, politicians, health professionals, actors, business leaders and so on). They are primarily unqualified, or their professional qualifications are not relevant to their online personas. They aspire to turn their personal social media profiles into professional commercial outlets.

Online, the ability to curate and present ourselves a certain way, and for those presentations to be seen by many, has led people like Anne and James to develop a certain aesthetic: a look and feel that embodies the identity they want to create. For Anne, this is a 'perfect mum' aesthetic; for James, it's 'gym-fit model'. There are 'travel guru' aesthetics, 'luxury lifestyle' aesthetics, 'foodie' aesthetics, 'festival' aesthetics, 'musically minded' aesthetics and so on. By giving influencers the ability to project and perform, and robust tools to manage this performance, online platforms offer exposure to groups and circles they want to reach: professional contacts, like-minded individuals. There is a social networking aspect (some may say social climbing) to certain platforms, particularly Instagram.

For others, however, the preening and posing have led to more anxiety and feelings of exposure. Social media can give rise to the same insecurities we had as adolescents, when we were self-consciously presenting a version of ourselves we thought might get the best responses, seeking validation and fearing judgement.

Sherry Turkle is a clinical psychologist and a professor of social science at the Massachusetts Institute of Technology who studies how technology impacts on society. Turkle's interviews with thirteen- to eighteen-year-olds reveal how much time they typically spend on their online profiles, creating and performing an identity. Adolescent soul-searching and identity construction are 'recast in terms of profile production'. Some have mastered the ability to create multiple profiles, each showing different versions of themselves, depending on the intended audience. There is a profile for university applications, one for an employer, one for the parents, and the profile only friends can see. 'Creating the illusion of authenticity demands virtuosity ... [it] is no easy work.'[6]

The challenge of constructing a profile online is that every act becomes a trade-off in curation and content management. Which photo should I post? Should I tag this person in it? Should I seek their permission first? Is a photograph or a comment the best expression of my thought? Did that quote I saw yesterday capture it better? Should I post while I'm angry, or wait until I'm not?

For some teens – and many adults – this 'production mindset' is too much work. It may come as no surprise that about 90 per cent of internet users are lurkers, who view, read and scroll others' content, but hardly post any of their own.[7] This is a variant of the well-known Pareto principle, which holds that 20 per cent of a group produces 80 per cent of the activity. Most simply find that staying up to date with their friends and families' activities and reading the odd interesting article is demanding enough. Yet even for viewers, the effects can be insidious.

Viewers are the recipient of the filtered, curated content from others. Each image and post suggests something about how bodies, people, places and lives should appear, and the effect on the viewer is cumulative. On visual platforms such as Instagram, 'influencers' present idealised lifestyles, often featuring exotic locations – whether a beautiful island overseas or a grand hotel lobby in their home city – and unattainable standards of beauty and body image. Even their 'mundane' daily activities (waking up, drinking a morning coffee, getting dressed) are carefully curated, while at the same time the illusion of unmediated access offers viewers a false sense of intimacy. For the viewer, what begins as casual browsing can easily escalate until social media becomes a bad habit. From there, it can be just a few clicks to neurosis. US psychologist George C. Boeree defines neurosis as a 'poor ability to adapt to one's environment, an inability to change one's life patterns, and the inability to develop a richer, more complex, more satisfying personality' – it is not difficult to see how this could develop in connection with an online platform based around lifestyle and personality.[8]

While the advertising industry is governed by certain standards and guidelines, platforms like Instagram have blurred the lines between organic content – ordinary posts by regular people, not meant to be promotional in nature – and advertisements. Some companies that have previously had limited avenues for advertising have seized on this. Take the questionable case of female gun influencers on Instagram, which generated enormous community outcry in 2019. Many online platforms don't allow gun advertisements, for obvious reasons.

On Instagram, personal profiles are not subject to the same restrictions as business profiles. Gun manufacturers found a grey area in 'influencer' content, where they could pay models to pose with guns the way a fashion house would their newest clothing line and luxury handbags. 'Influencers' like Kimberly Matte post 'thirst traps'. The difference was that for a fee she was happy to include a shot of herself posing with an AR battle rifle. Lauren Young has posted professionally produced photos that look like they belong in a homewares catalogue, except instead of holding up cute knick-knacks and crafts, she's balancing an enormous machine gun on her hip. While this practice has now been banned, it took pressure from tech critics and the public before Instagram took action. No doubt new types of influencers will continue to emerge as companies find new ways of exploiting the platform.

'Influencer' started to become a viable career sometime after 2010, as the social media platforms grew exponentially in size and reach, and everyday people with specific interests found they could build an audience of followers. Companies and brands saw opportunities in reaching niche audiences in categories such as beauty, health, fitness, travel, food and culture, and began to include influencers as part of their outreach campaigns, commercial sponsorships and partnerships. But to this day, it is difficult to quantify an influencer's actual 'influence' on a company's bottom line. Often, they are merely cheaper, readily available content producers who charge less for a professional-looking shoot than industry agencies.

But the effect is insidious, as studies are beginning to reveal that influencer culture has made shallower people out of mothers like Anne, egotists out of gym junkies like James and fragile neurotics out the rest of us. The superficial presentation of ideal lives, body types and selves is leading to the manifestation of psychological disorders.

In the United States, there are approximately 30 million people who suffer from an eating disorder. In Australia, that figure is around 1 million.[9] Teenage girls and young women are the largest group of sufferers, and for good reason have received the bulk of the media's attention – it is estimated that 63 per cent of people with eating disorders in Australia are female. A topic that receives less attention is that gay men make up a disproportionate number of people suffering from disordered eating relative to population size.[10] For many gay men, an ideal body type is a requirement if they want to be seen as belonging to 'the gay scene'. Instagram influencers regularly post semi-nude selfies, and only ever pose with other similarly buff men. This 'aesthetic' perpetuates unhealthy stereotypes and can contribute to an individual's development of disordered eating patterns.

Body dysmorphia can also take other forms. Some influencers and their followers have taken the pressure to maintain an unrealistic standard of beauty to the extreme, electing for cosmetic surgery so they look more like the filtered, edited and airbrushed versions of themselves. Dubbed 'selfie dysmorphia', men and women as young as nineteen are undergoing major surgery to make them look more like their digitally enhanced selves. The American Academy of Facial Plastic and Reconstructive Surgery surveyed its members and found that 55 per cent of surgeons reported seeing patients who gave their motivation as wanting to 'look better in selfies'.[11] There is also the phenomenon of 'Barbie dolls'. Melbourne resident Tara Jayne McConachy – who has claimed 'we just want to look like an edited photo in real life' – has spent $135,000 on cosmetic surgery to grossly enhance her lips and breasts, among other features. McConachy, who joined controversial platform OnlyFans to help fund future cosmetic work, says she 'loves her plastic doll vibe' and is considering enhancing her E-cup breasts further. (OnlyFans is a content subscription service where influencers can sell images directly to their fanbase.) Amanda Ahola, a Finnish woman, almost died after a 2018 breast augmentation when she suffered a seizure. Her surgery was reportedly 'partially paid for by a sugar daddy who approached her via Instagram'.[12]

Sherry Turkle writes that in the psychoanalytic tradition, narcissism isn't interpreted in the way we commonly see it depicted – that is, as a condition where people love themselves a little too much. She explains that it's about 'a personality so fragile that it needs constant support. It cannot tolerate the complex demands of other people but trie[s] to relate to them by distorting who they are and splitting off what [they] need, what [they] can use. So the narcissistic self gets on with others by dealing only with their made-to-measure representations. These representations … are all that the fragile self can handle.' Influencer culture is an unfortunate symptom of an unhealthy relationship with online representation, and for those suffering from narcissism, it can be downright dangerous.

In September 2021, Facebook, Inc. (now called Meta) was subjected to a series of damning leaks. Former employee turned whistleblower Frances Haugen leaked thousands of pages of internal documents showcasing a breadth of extremely serious issues with Facebook and Instagram – including ignoring human rights abuses such as human trafficking and failing to act on local terrorist groups. One of the key revelations was that the company knew how toxic Instagram was for teenage girls. Its own research had found that 13 per cent of British teen users and 6 per cent of American teen users traced the source of their suicidal thoughts to Instagram. Moreover, 32 per cent of teen girls and 14 per cent of teen boys said Instagram made them feel worse about their bodies. 'We make body image issues worse for one in three teen girls,' a summary of the research said.[13] This research came as Facebook wanted to attract younger users to its ageing platforms (according to the Pew Research Center, use of Facebook has declined 39 per cent among those aged thirteen to seventeen since 2014–15)[14] and was never made public.

What is happening is a larger trend in how online representation is changing our relationship with reality, fuelled by influencers and the platforms themselves. On Instagram, users can view someone's 'highlights' and compare it to their own. A highlight reel is overwhelmingly envy-inducing, a wet-dream polaroid of what life ought to be. It is travel without the sixteen-hour flight, the fit body without the six-days-a-week workout regime and birthday parties without the crying baby. These approximations of reality start to become our new normal. As we edit out the messiness and ugliness of real life, we begin to forget that this messiness and ugliness exists for others too. We accept approximations of life *as* life. Online, we start accepting things that are 'real enough'. And if this pattern of thinking takes hold of us, we begin to feel that our lives should reflect an Instagram feed, rather than the other way around.

Reality is flat, 'real enough' is better

Disney's Animal Kingdom, a zoological park dedicated to the theme of animal protection and conservation, opened in Orlando, Florida, in 1998. It houses live animals. Some of its early visitors complained that the live animals weren't 'realistic' enough. What they meant was that the live animals did not behave like the robotic animals at Disney World. The robotic crocodiles slapped their tails and rolled their eyes, being very 'crocodile-like', while the real crocodiles mainly baked motionless in the sun. It was all very disappointing to come expecting action and encounter sloth.

While this seems absurd, it belies our willingness to accept simulations as reality. Crocodiles are *supposed* to be crocodile-like and display crocodile behaviour on cue, for our viewing pleasure – never mind that most of us have never seen a crocodile out in the wild, or spent time observing their behaviour, and so have limited information on which to base this belief. On Instagram, a successful children's birthday party is *supposed* to be flawlessly decorated, with an amazing-looking cake and constantly smiling guests. A desirable young man is *supposed* to be bronzed, buffed and cosmopolitan – hey, even the ancient Greeks knew it. That's what people want to see, that's what generates an audience.

Online, the ability to curate and perform 'our best lives' can have even broader implications. As we scroll through beautiful sunsets on faraway islands, and click 'like' on bronze, sculpted bodies, a sumptuously set dinner table or a perfectly coordinated outfit, we start to forget about the moments in life that are not post-worthy. This has been referred to as 'flat time'. Flat time is the period in between remarkable moments, which passes uncelebrated and undocumented. Flat time is where life just happens. Our relationships, our work and our lives continue along, and all is gradual, slow, for the most part pleasantly uneventful.

Online, flat time does not exist. We scroll through abridged versions of each other's lives, each milestone giving way to the next. We scroll from one holiday to another, the start of a course to its end, the beginning of a relationship through to marriage and children and, sometimes, divorce, new partners and new children. Even the format for Instagram Reels reflects this idea of a highlight reel. The most interesting article won't be read unless it is beneath an eye-catching, pithy headline. The most sophisticated movie needs to be distilled into a punchy thirty-second trailer. Online, the pace of life becomes exaggerated, sped up, until flat time (otherwise known as reality) feels, well, flat.

Social Media 1.0 was about building community and participatory features into a previously static internet. Back then, this meant blogs, Wikipedia pages, comments and discussion forums. It allowed people to communicate, collaborate and connect. It allowed for an exchange of ideas and conversation, rather than a one-way broadcast from producer to consumer. Before it became the commoditised version we know today, social media seemed to genuinely be about communication.

As Social Media 1.0 matured into Social Media 2.0, commerciality entered the picture. Companies noticed the vast number of people (potential 'audiences') gathering around topics they enjoyed. Why couldn't those topics be linked to their products and services? With this commodification of social media, we adopted the lingo. We measured our profiles like they were companies, enumerating production value, scale, reach and engagement. (The great irony is that for companies, social media was an opportunity to 'become more human'. Workshops developed around 'humanising your brand' to better appeal to the public. I have conducted some of these workshops myself, so I say this with a complete lack – well, okay, just a pinch – of judgement.) In the process, though, users became more like companies. Having adopted the tools and metrics of commerce and industry, many allowed themselves to become walking advertisements. They started to treat life as either post-worthy or not. If a woman is a stylish and savvy mother, why wouldn't she dress her child (and herself) in outfits that may prompt a clothing company to come knocking with a sponsorship deal? A young man is attractive and fit and works hard to maintain his physique, so why wouldn't he post about his gym sessions in case a health supplements company might want to sponsor these sessions?

But in aspiring to become captains of our own industry, we can start to get confused about the boundaries between friends and fans. We can start to blur the lines between our real lives, our real relationships and ones that seem 'real enough'. We can start to question if our experiences are worthwhile if they aren't being validated by our networks. In 2011, Dale Carnegie, the celebrated author of *How to Win Friends and Influence People*, updated his classic work for our digital times. In it, he explores the idea of 'real enough' friends: 'So often we are content to simply plug others into our digital world and browse them like commodities until we are ready to engage in some sort of transaction. Such sentiment removes the nobility inherent in our shared humanity. It makes our relationships merely tools for transaction rather than transcendence.'[15]

When we begin to treat each other as commodities, and accept only approximations of our lives, we miss the simple truths about each other. Online, we cannot read a person's face and their 'nuances of feeling'. That experience doesn't allow for 'passively being yourself' – that is, being who you are 'when you are not trying, not performing'. For Sherry Turkle, simulation 'demands immersion [and] creates a self that prefers simulation'.[16] Online, relationships might be simpler, more controlled, and better-looking, but the simulations miss a lot.

Positive online representations

There are of course positive effects that come from online representation. Representations are about identity and about power, and social media gives many the power to declare their own voice, to demand to be heard, to tell their story (or at least Instagram Story) in the way they want it told. Before the internet, our collective stories, our histories, were written only by those who had the means and the incentive to do so. These authors told stories that were inevitably limited in scope and substance – they selected tales that would appeal mostly to their own constituents or reflected only their own experiences and those of others like them. Online, we can write, post and share our own stories, told the way we want. Of course there will be noise. A cacophony of a billion people's voices is at once astounding, overwhelming, chaotic and invigorating.

Australian non-profit R U OK? resulted from a son's struggle. Gavin Larkin ran a successful advertising agency and had a loving family of a wife and three children. But his father's suicide had left many painful unanswered questions. Determined to play a role in the battle against suicide, Gavin developed R U OK? Day. The idea was to create an opportunity for people to reach out and have a conversation with friends, loved ones, even strangers. The simple act of asking, 'Are you okay?' could help save a life. It was based on the insight that many people who are at risk of harming themselves, especially men, feel disconnected and have no one to confide in.

I was fortunate enough to be one of the early digital strategists for R U OK? Day. I got involved in 2010 when the agency I worked for took this on as a pro-bono project. R U OK? Day back then was a great concept with some excellent communication and design collateral (thanks to Gavin's advertising agency) but limited reach. What it did have was a core idea that was unique and very translatable online. In its early days, R U OK? did not fundraise. In fact, it didn't really consider itself a charity, more a grassroots movement. It simply wanted you to reach out and have a potentially life-saving conversation with someone else.

The online strategy was critical to the early growth of R U OK? The internet was a cost-effective way of spreading the message. We developed bold designs for R U OK? Day digital ribbons and profile photo attachments, the kind that are now commonplace in cause-related campaigns but at the time were innovative. We used social media to spread the word and share the hashtag, which trended nationwide. We asked receptive Australian celebrities to film low-cost videos that could be shared online. An R U OK? Day digital ribbon became not only about spreading the word but a unique identifier, meaning you were open to having a conversation with someone who might need it. R U OK? Day soon grew into a national movement, with a 78 per cent awareness among Australians by 2017. It is no exaggeration to say that millions of potentially life-saving conversations may have happened as a result. I believe it would not have gained the traction it did without the internet, and I am proud to have been a small contributor to that success. R U OK? Day represented a desire to take mental health seriously and offered people a signal for connection. It was a display of compassion and empathy for fellow humans. R U OK? Day has since been subject to both praise and criticism, but there is no doubt that its vision of elevating a simple idea to national awareness came to fruition.

#MeToo, a social movement against sexual abuse, sexual harassment and rape culture, is a clear example of the power of social media (and celebrity). Social activist Tarana Burke began using the phrase as early as 2006, but it wasn't until actress Alyssa Milano tweeted it in 2017 as a call to action that it gained widespread popularity. The hashtag #MeToo became a rallying cry for the many women who shared stories of abuse and called out those responsible for them. It was at once a protest, a declaration, a call to arms, a demand for justice and an extended hand. The hashtag was used by more than 4.7 million people in 12 million posts, comments and reactions on Facebook in the first twenty-four hours. Facebook reported that 45 per cent of users in the United States had a friend who had posted using the hashtag within a year. On Twitter, the hashtag was tweeted more than 19 million times in the first twelve months.[17]

A study by researcher John Ayres from the University of California, San Diego, revealed that searches related to reporting sexual harassment and assault were up 30 per cent, and searches related to training to prevent harassment and assault were up 50 per cent, in the months after Milano's tweet.[18] Many sought out assistance after posting. The National Women's Law Center created a fund in the wake of the movement. 'Since then, over 3,800 people have reached out to us seeking assistance for workplace sexual harassment. People send us requests for assistance online, and so it does seem like people are using online tools. We've received many more requests for assistance than we ever thought we would receive,' said Sharyn Tejani, director of Time's Up Legal Defense Fund.[19]

The movement has since caused a chain reaction worldwide that has seen men in powerful positions removed and, in the United States, the signing into law of a Congressional '#MeToo bill', which aims to improve the process for sexual harassment complaints and allegations in the workplace. Around the world the movement continues, with local campaigns and legislative reforms. #MeToo became a representation for equality, justice and strength.

Both R U OK? and #MeToo tapped into a larger phenomenon that online platforms have facilitated. On social media, individuals can personalise and broadcast their interest in certain causes and movements. Anthropologist Sally Engle Merry calls this 'vernacularisation', whereby individuals, groups and communities translate human rights concepts into their own terms and communicate them through their own stories, breathing new life into campaigns that have historically been led by human rights groups, governments and NGOs.[20] Both R U OK? and #MeToo allow for a kind of global language of participation. If identity is performative and developed over time, movements like R U OK? and #MeToo add dimensions of compassion, connection and social justice to our online selves.

How to be authentic online

Are we destined for a world where we become fully 'transparent', where our most private moments are broadcast for all to see, or can we continue to value our experiences without the social validation we gain by posting about them? Will our lives become merely content, as we devalue everyday moments that aren't deemed post-worthy, warping our sense of real life? While we cannot say where social media will take our society, we do have choice and agency as to how (and whether) we use it.

Every post we make involves a conscious decision about how we present ourselves online. What we post may be superficial or vain, or it can be empowering and do broader good. We can choose to present ourselves as vapid influencers, valuing inauthentic approximations of life, or we can seek to cultivate authentic online representations, which draw on community, real emotions and real relationships. That's not to say we can never post something frivolous or silly, but the version of self we create on our Instagram and Facebook feeds should be recognisable to us *as* us. The balance of real life to manufactured content should always fall on the side of glorious, messy, mundane reality.

What we should strive for is an online experience where our representations of ourselves and our choices around that representation are as healthy and minimally harmful as possible, both for our own sake and for others'. This means being aware of the impact of what we post and being mindful of not skewing or distorting our content, lest we start to believe in a distorted view of reality.

What can individuals do?

Recognise that social media profiles are only snapshots

The constant barrage of content on social media, and the way that Instagram, Facebook and Twitter encourage endless scrolling, can short-circuit our brains. Too much time spent looking at others' profiles may make us think we are viewing reality instead of approximations of it.

Social media feeds are carefully curated, algorithmically enhanced products and do not reflect the full spectrum of a person's identity. The first step in transitioning from being a passive to an active consumer of content is understanding their design and their limits. We mustn't compare our lives to curated feeds because the two are not the same. We mustn't fool ourselves into thinking that Instagram can give us a real insight to that person's thoughts, failures and achievements. Social media feeds are just a series of snapshots, moments in time, often with little context and therefore questionable value. Keeping this front of mind every time we log in will help change how we approach social media content.

Learn to unfollow

Facebook has hijacked the word 'friend'. RSVPs have become merely signs of good intentions. Active communication has given way to passive stalking. And spending time with people has been compromised by spending time looking at social media profiles.

A tenuous relationship with 'the real' can lead users to confuse between genuine relationships and acquaintances. 'Dunbar's number' is a concept which states that humans are only able to maintain about 150 relationships – the size of a small tribe. Social media has complicated this with its capacity to foster virtual relationships, but the theory holds a persistent truth – we cannot maintain meaningful relationships at a certain scale. As we engage with others online, it's worth being clear about who our real friends are and who are merely followers. The number of followers does not equal the amount of meaningful interaction.

Periodically reassess who you follow on social media and why. Is an influencer offering valuable advice and insights or just posting pretty pictures that make you feel bad about yourself? Do you think about their content when you're offline? Does it serve you to comment on others' posts if you are only doing so to seek their approval? What are you gaining from these interactions – and what are you losing?

If social media is beginning to make you question your self-worth or warp your idea of relationships, body image and lifestyle, then perhaps it's time to unfollow. Influencers, some of whom are engaged in an unhealthy cycle of posting due to a pressure to broadcast regularly to their followers and keep up their audience figures, might even benefit from your disengagement. A decreasing audience for their harmful content could be the most constructive feedback of all.

Ultimately, it's worth asking yourself the question: does following this person add value to my life?

Keep some things offline

It might seem blatantly obvious that there is value in being selective about what you post, when and why. But many young people, screen addicts and even professionals who work in and with social media can feel pressured to post as much as they can about their lives and thoughts online. Whether it's to fit in with their peer group, or because they don't recognise the addictive nature of algorithms (which are designed to maximise time spent on the platform), or whether it's become a measure of their self-worth or professional success, many people slip into the habit of obsessively posting content, often without forethought or insight.

More content does not mean a fuller life – if anything, the opposite may be true. An event or a memorable moment is no less important if does not appear on social media. And sometimes, a quick tweet or comment that may seem witty or mildly controversial at the time can have far-reaching negative consequences.

If you are a serial poster, try to work out what you gain from it. Are you addicted to the dopamine hits of instant reaction? Who are you posting content for? Does it need to be said or shown? What value does it offer your followers? Aim to cut down the number of posts you make in a typical week, either by a certain percentage or by making the decision to only post with deliberation and thought, when something strikes you as worthy. You may find that posting less often will make a positive difference to the quality of both your life and your profile.

Disconnect or take a social media break

Research has demonstrated that taking breaks from social media can improve wellbeing, depression and anxiety.[21] The idea of 'disconnecting' might seem obvious and simple, but it is a lot easier said than done. The reality is that much of our lives is mediated by digital technology and our smartphones are irritatingly useful devices that now house so much utility – our contacts, our bank accounts, our entertainment, our shopping, our news, our work and more. Disconnecting, therefore, needs to be a conscious and deliberate effort, but there are different tactics that could help.

- **Turn on features that limit usage.** Many smartphones now come with features that limit your time spent on certain apps. You can set up time limits; when you reach that limit, some apps send alerts, while others shut the app down.
- **Turn off notifications.** Notifications keep us in a constant state of alertness and attentiveness, providing a stream of stimulus which keeps you hooked to your device. Turning these off could help with curbing social media usage.
- **Schedule offline times.** Meal breaks, the hour before going to bed, or any other appropriate moment where you don't need your phone could assist you in creating routines and habits where social media usage is limited.
- **Disentangle functions from your phone.** Do you really need to use your smart wallet or Apple Pay for transactions? Do you really need the Opal or Myki app, rather than the physical card, to board public transport? Do you really need to download every app suggested to you? Disentangling utilities from your smartphone may help to limit online connectivity.

These are only some suggestions of ways to disconnect, which could help make the use of social media healthier and more manageable. But ultimately, what we need is to develop online spaces and platforms that we shouldn't need to deliberately disconnect from. Our digital world should not be built with addiction and entrapment in mind, and it shouldn't be up to individuals to spend so much effort fighting against unhealthy digital products. What we need more than individual actions are system-wide interventions.

What can governments and society do?

Regulate social media influencers

A key problem with social media is that influencers have been allowed to flourish with few rules around what they can post, when or how often. While traditional publishers and advertising channels must comply with a diverse range of regulations and codes, and are overseen by various regulatory bodies, these safeguards do not apply to social media influencers. Some influencers rise to the status of celebrity – it is not uncommon for Australian influencers to have hundreds of thousands of followers. As the impact of online influencers on society in general increases, some are generating substantial income – if online reports that Kylie Jenner can command $1,000,000 or more for a sponsored post are true, influencers who are raking in even one-fortieth of that are doing very well indeed. They should be subject to the same regulations as any other commercial business. We could start with the below at a minimum.

- **Regulation parity between influencer advertising and mainstream advertising.** Many influencers 'collaborate' with brands and charge thousands of dollars for a sponsored post endorsing a product. These influencers should have to abide by the same codes of conduct as mainstream advertisers, which aim to ensure certain safety and ethical standards. This includes restrictions on advertising alcohol to minors and junk food to children.

There are also restrictions on body image advertising, particularly if targeted to young people. A report by the Centre for Responsible Technology found the glaring disparity between influencer advertising and other equivalent advertising. For example, in the health and wellness category there are no less than fifteen codes and regulations for businesses, while influencers only have to comply with three loose codes; these are general in nature and not designed specifically for influencer activity.[22] Regulatory bodies such as the Australian Competition and Consumer Commission and the Australian Securities and Investments Commission can invest in clear frameworks that include due reference to social media influencers. Some moves have been made towards this. Under laws that came into effect on 1 July 2022, the Australian Therapeutic Goods Administration has banned social media influencers from promoting health products, including medical devices and medications, if the influencer is being paid or incentivised, including receiving gifted products. This is a welcome move in a regulatory environment that, until recently, has given little attention to influencers.

- **Strong and enforceable regulations.** Even where there are guidelines in place, some advertising codes leave the industry responsible for enforcement. Some social media influencers may not realise they need to abide by these codes, as they do not consider themselves to be 'advertisers'. For example, the Australian Association of National Advertisers' Code of Ethics specifies: 'Advertising must not portray an unrealistic ideal body image by portraying body shapes or features that are unrealistic or unattainable through healthy practices.'[23] While this code does apply to social media content, it is self-regulatory. It is likely that many social media influencers, unless they have undertaken training in advertising standards or have educated themselves on the topic, are not even aware of its existence. Clear regulations, overseen by regulatory bodies and with significant penalties and fines for non-compliance, are generally more effective than self-regulatory codes.

- **Qualifications to advertise products in certain categories.** Australian law professor Vicky Waye notes, 'Influencers have become an important marketing tool because they are perceived by many to be genuine and credible sources of information about product quality. However, the incentives that influencers receive from the companies that supply the products or services they promote are rarely disclosed and influencers may have little basis or few credentials for some of the claims made. Consumers of the products can therefore be misled.'[24] This is of particular concern with sensitive topics such as finance (overseen by the Australian Securities and Investments Commission), as a slew of influencers can post information and make recommendations without any formal finance-related qualifications or experience. Rules around qualifications, certifications and professional licences, which grant the holder the authority to speak on certain topics, must extend to the online space as well as the physical. By creating stricter rules and frameworks around influencers, we can ensure a healthier and more accurate ecosystem of content.

- **Deplatforming bad actors.** Some influencers have an evangelical streak and feel compelled to provide their followers with their views on vaccinations and medications, or offer investment advice, or recommend pyramid schemes – even when they are not being paid for it. There are numerous examples of influencers posting dangerous and often illegal content (particularly around vaccination during the pandemic). We need a stricter system to punish bad actors. Social media platforms, which for too long have avoided their social responsibility to moderate problematic content, must step up. Users need to be better monitored by these companies and banned when they break the rules.

- **Deprioritising quantity metrics as measures of success.** Influencers first gained traction because they had sizeable followings that could be marketed to. But their conversion rates (whether they can convince their followers to purchase a specific product or use a particular service) are often very poor. Not all influencers are actually able to 'influence' their followers – who are mostly passive. Any company, agency or brand engaging influencers should insist on quality metrics, such as conversion rates, rather than vanity metrics, such as number of followers. Companies should also question whether it's worth engaging with influencers at all, if success rates are so variable and there are no agreed-upon benchmarks for quality or standards in the influencer industry. Shifting our measures of success from quantity (followers, likes per post) to quality (purchase conversions, action conversions and referrals) will go a long way towards determining the true value of influencer engagement.

Provide better mental health services for those affected by social media

Vulnerable groups on social media – teens, those with anxiety and depression, and those with body-image issues, including body dysmorphia – are having unhealthy experiences on Instagram, YouTube and TikTok. Often, the content they engage with on these platforms can reinforce or enhance their negative thought patterns and behaviours. We must provide better mental health services to support such people. This could include awareness campaigns around the potential harms of social media. Such programs and campaigns could guide participants through asking the kinds of questions we should all ask of social media: are their online relationships toxic? Is serial posting or endless scrolling a sign of dependence? Does their time on social media make them feel worse about themselves?

Social media is a pervasive part of our lives. We must provide users with the psychological tools and resources to navigate an online world, to ensure that everyone's digital experience is as safe and healthy as possible.

––––––––––

Just as the fable of Narcissus warned, we mustn't be dazzled by shiny and intoxicating surfaces that lack depth. Social media is a mirror that reflects both the best and the worst of ourselves. It may be a tool for good, if we focus on its community-building aspects and present ourselves with authenticity, showing our flaws as well as our strengths. But if we fall in love with our own reflections, we will become shallower versions of ourselves.

The Hateful Troll

Does an insult become less offensive because it's on Twitter? Does a cruel zinger become funnier because your followers read it on your Instagram?

Here's a question: have you ever had a fight with someone on social media? I've got into online battles with people for the most inane reasons, like what someone was wearing or their reaction to a movie, as well as for consequential things, such as climate action or geopolitics. If you have an account on a public social network, or have commented on public websites, chances are you have too.

Now imagine yourself having that same argument with someone face-to-face. I'm almost certain that it wouldn't result in the same heated back-and-forth. It may even resolve in an entirely different way.

Online, there are those who make provocative, rude or hostile comments to elicit an emotional response. They purposefully cause fights and stir up trouble. We call these people 'trolls'.

There was a time around the early 2000s when trolling was mostly about humour and satire, about responding to people in a sardonic way for laughs, rather than throwing insults and inciting sledging matches. But these days trolling has become synonymous with abuse, hate speech and harassment. Certain groups even coordinate online abuse to deliberately target and do harm to their victims.

'Trolling' has become an umbrella term for spouting hatred and abuse online. Trolling can sometimes be confused with legitimate criticism, where the subject of the critique dislikes it and dismisses the critic as a 'troll'. Other times, it includes criminal acts, targeted harassment and violence that spills over into the physical world. As we will see in this chapter, the spectrum of 'trolling behaviour' has become wide, from negative comments about someone, to posts from groups labelled as terrorist organisations, to online activity from neo-Nazis, who have found that many trolls are ripe for recruitment to their causes. The common thread with trolling is hate and abuse through online commentary.

Alarmingly, a study conducted by the Australia Institute found that more than one-third of Australians have experienced some form of online harassment or abuse, and that this has become a frequent, almost unavoidable, phenomenon for many groups and individuals online. Let's go trawling for trolls.

Trolls and their targets

As far as online abuse goes, Carly Findlay has experienced it all – jokes, mockery, insults, gaslighting and death threats. The author of the memoir *Say Hello* (2019), who describes herself as a 'writer, speaker, appearance activist', consistently demonstrates strength and grace online despite the trolling she has been subjected to. She has even managed to turn her trolling experiences online into something productive that strengthens her advocacy.

Carly was born with a rare painful genetic skin condition called ichthyosis, which causes her skin to have a red, scaly appearance.

The treatment she uses also makes her skin very shiny. Having grown up with this condition, she is sadly familiar with the range of reactions it can cause in others. But the internet turbocharged other people's ability to have a say about her appearance.

One pivotal moment in her relationship with the internet came in 2013. She had started blogging around 2010 to share her experiences and provide information about her skin condition. Back then, she was reluctant to post photos of herself online, as she was acutely aware that some might make fun of her. But after a steady stream of support from her readers, she grew more confident about sharing photos. Then, in December 2013, she woke up to a large surge in traffic to her blog, all before 7.00 am. She knew something had happened. After checking the source of the traffic, she discovered that it was from the online platform Reddit. One of her worst fears had come to pass – someone had found a photo of her online and shared it as a target for ridicule.

A sense of dread settled on her as she investigated a public forum called 'What the Fuck'. Some of the comments were horrible. I will not reproduce the worst of them here, but to give a sense of their vileness:

Lobster

She looks like a glazed donut

WTF is that? Looks like something that was partially digested by my dog.

Seeing people like this smile makes me uncomfortable. It looks like a lie; they are only smiling in an attempt to fool themselves that their lives aren't horrible. You can see it in her eyes. The same rehearsed dead-eye mouth-smile in all her pictures. Gives me the willies.

There were many who (incorrectly) diagnosed her condition and many assumptions of sunburn, which irritated her. There was even one that said she 'should be killed with fire'. But Carly forced herself to keep reading, and among the hateful, ignorant comments she found some who called out the trolls, others who wanted to learn more about her condition and still more who defended her even though they had no idea that she would read them doing so.

She decided to post a response on the thread:

> I knew the day would come that someone would create a Reddit thread about me, using my photo, having a laugh at my appearance.
>
> For years, that fear was why I didn't share photos of me online. But now, after gaining confidence and support through years of blogging, I couldn't care whether they call me a lobster or silly putty.
>
> The love I have around me and success I have had through telling my own story to break down stigma like these Reddit threads is stronger than any of those words.
>
> Yes I have Ichthyosis. Yes that picture is me. Don't fear it and don't criticise it. I am proud of the way I look, what I have achieved and for telling my story.
>
> FYI: I have two forms of Ichthyosis – a mix of Netherton's syndrome and erythroderma. My skin is shiny because I use paraffin. My body is less red than my face as it's not exposed to the elements, but it is generally more painful. Ichthyosis is survivable – I have lived a very full life.
>
> Thanks for linking to my blog too, so people are informed of the real me rather than through the speculation on this thread.

For those who missed it, you can read more about me at *http://carlyfindlay.blogspot.com* [1]

Instantly the tone of the thread changed. Strangers rushed to congratulate her, thank her for her strength and celebrate her blog and the way it educated people about her condition. This Bostonite was one: 'You, madam, are the strongest motherfucker I have ever HEARD of, let alone met. If you are ever in boston, i would be honored to buy you a beer.' Even the original poster gave her an apology (sort of).

This mix of abuse and support is a regular occurrence for Carly, who can get death threats and date requests in the same breath on her online channels. These days, she's a successful and fierce advocate for disability and appearance diversity, and she speaks and writes regularly about the harms of trolling and online abuse.

For Carly, it's important not to differentiate between 'real life' and 'online' because they are both environments in which people interact. As a writer and blogger, social media platforms are 'an extension' of her workplace, and they are often unsafe spaces. She believes the moderation of content on the Big Tech social media platforms is woefully inadequate, as she sees a continuous tirade of hate speech against disabled people get through so-called community standard policies. Sometimes, disabled people's bodies and faces are even incorrectly moderated and removed entirely. Instagram accounts such as Special Books by Special Kids, which aims to spread support and awareness for disabled people around the world, routinely gets a 'sensitive content warning' posted on its photos. It's not just people who discriminate; now internet algorithms do as well.

And while Carly's story is one of triumph and grit, there are those who have not been so lucky. Television presenter Charlotte Dawson committed suicide in her Sydney home in 2014 and was referred to in the media as the 'first celebrity victim of trolling'. She had a history of battling trolls on Twitter. As she tried to fight back she became a bigger target, and eventually the relentless abuse became too much.

There are many more women (and yes, it hardly needs to be said, but women get a disproportionate amount of the abuse) with public profiles who have called out trolls, including journalists Tracey Spicer, Leigh Sales and Erin Molan, but for every privileged woman with support and a platform, there are thousands with stories that go unreported, many of whom are young and have not built up a support system. Some simply cannot cope with the abuse and suffer irreparable trauma, or even take their own lives.

Abuse online has very real consequences, and trolls are conscious of this. There is a range of reasons for why trolls do what they do.

Ginger Gorman wrote a seminal book on trolls called *Troll Hunting*, which examines the psychology of the online troll. In it she spoke to a range of men who gave various reasons to explain their trolling.

Mark was 'unremarkable in the extreme' – the kind of guy you would pass on the street and forget immediately. But underneath the banal façade was a cold, calculating and committed troll. He trolled people online because he liked to hurt others. For Mark, and the troll syndicate he was a member of, baiting people and getting a reaction was fun. He enjoyed making people feel unsafe online. He would troll rape victims, debase the Facebook memorials of those who had committed suicide and target those with autism or mental illnesses. In other words, Mark was a vile human being. But he would never classify himself as one. For Mark, his trolling was 'just for lulz'.

Craig, by contrast, was polite, measured and generous in explaining to Gorman the ins and outs of trolling behaviour. Craig preyed on people in positions of power – public figures, politicians, business leaders, journalists. Craig saw Mark's version of trolling as 'abuse', not 'legitimate trolling'. For him, trolling was about winding people up for political reasons, almost a way to provoke accountability or level the playing field. His trolling started as a means to vent his political frustrations. Twitter became a megaphone for him to call out wrongs. He realised the reactions he would provoke in making provocative statements such as 'The NBN is a waste of money'. The gulf between the two men, who could both be classified as 'trolls' but whose motivations and approaches were in stark contrast, is wide.

Among Gorman's case studies, one character stands out – his online alias is Meepsheep. Meepsheep gained notoriety by hacking Hillary Clinton's Wikipedia page and replacing it with porn and a pro-Trump message in 2016. He became known among troll circles and was admired by many trolls, new and experienced. He was also president of a trolling group that was labelled a 'cyberterrorist organisation' by the Terrorism Research & Analysis Consortium. Meepsheep suggested that for many trolls, the 'internet was [their] parent'. With little supervision during their formative years, sometime between puberty and their late teens they found the internet. They would spend hours on forums like 4chan and Tumblr. These young (and usually white) men were filled with rage, confusion and frustration, and were allowed to roam free in an online landscape with almost no rules and no accountability. Therefore, a kind of radicalisation took place, a hardening of behaviour. Meepsheep describes a world of 'emotional poverty', a world that 'makes you feel like you're worth absolutely nothing and it tears you up inside for years, and then you find an outlet with people who understand and agree, and it's also the only place you've ever found that'.

His organisation used various trolling methods. These include crapflooding – flooding a website's comments section, chat channels and forums with worthless text – creating malware and disrupting popular websites. These types of techniques indicate a coordinated, organised community, with active members who regularly assess the impact and effectiveness of their 'campaigns'. As it turns out, this is true of many other cyber hate groups. Far from being a disparate, motley collection, many are semi-professional in their methods and organisation.[2]

What does it take to become a troll who 'does it for the lulz', or one who becomes a leader of a terrorist organisation? One man, Michael, fell into the darkest versions of online abuse and radicalisation, becoming a fully fledged leader of a neo-Nazi gang.

————

Michael was the type of young man the internet loves to corrupt. He was smart, articulate and passionate, and he wanted to make change in the world. He was frustrated at the current system of politics and he wanted to do something about it. The internet took this seed and twisted it into something hateful.

Michael is from a middle-class white Australian family. He was a loner as a child, spending a lot of time by himself. His father, an active Liberal Party member who 'cared deeply for his country' and 'wanted to make it better', was a significant early influence on him. His father had strong views around politics, religion and patriotism. Michael adopted these views wholesale, and it left him with a hunger for conservative ideals.

His radicalisation happened around 2016. At that time, there was a focus on Islam and how it 'fitted in' with Western society. The world was grappling with the rise of ISIS – global terror attacks and local ones as well – and there was a rise in Islamophobia. Michael found the organisation Reclaim Australia and began attending their protests. There were some present who held white supremist beliefs.

And then, following a pattern that's sadly common among interviewees in this book, he found the internet. It turbocharged his radicalisation. He started interacting with conservative Facebook groups, and Facebook did what it did best – opened a firehose of similar content and pages that flooded his feed. Quickly, he found right-wing figures such as Milo Yiannopoulos, Paul Joseph Watson and Richard Spencer, who were pumping out hateful, racist propaganda. It was easy for him to find numerous YouTube channels showcasing racist and far-right views, such as Black Pigeon Speaks, which he felt had 'seriously good production values'. He fell into a black hole, as the content he consumed became more and more extreme.

On YouTube, he found extreme conspiracy theories, such as 'The Great Replacement Theory', which states that there is a vast conspiracy to replace Westernised, European-based culture and peoples with 'other' cultures, like Islam. This soup of disinformation and propaganda pushed a receptive Michael into extreme ring-wing ideology.

'There's definitely a grooming process,' he reflects. Through groups on Facebook, some users were actively propelling receptive youths towards more and more extreme ideology. 'Memes would get edgier, then link to more extreme groups, then those memes would get edgier and link to more extreme groups,' Michael said, and this process would repeat itself until suddenly he found himself far from a relatively banal group about Australian nationalism that posted

Australia Day jokes, where he had started, and on a page that espoused neo-Nazi ideology.

Michael was engaging frequently with a local Facebook group called 'Grass Roots Nationalism', whose administrator, Jake, started to test Michael's receptivity to more extreme views. It wasn't long before he was indoctrinated into neo-Nazi groups that were proudly fascist, explicitly racist and unashamedly violent. Members talked openly about influencing the political landscape, creating their own town as a hub for group members, and infiltrating political groups, in particular the National Party, One Nation and the Palmer United Party, to push hardline stances against immigration and in favour of a racist agenda.

Michael became a leading recruiter for these groups, drawing on his online savvy to create sophisticated recruitment and radicalisation 'funnels' using Facebook, 4chan, private messaging and memes. He would identify users online who were like him – young, with a lot of time on their hands and angry. Then, depending on their interests – nationalism, alpha-male dominance, anti-immigration policy – he would tailor his message to appeal, gradually introducing them to more and more extreme ideas and content, until they were ready to join a neo-Nazi group.

What is fascinating about Michael's story is that he is not a classic troll in the sense that he intentionally set out to abuse people online. Instead, it shows that the conditions that facilitate or incubate trolls are the same conditions that help radicalise other young men into extreme behaviour. 'Trolling' has evolved. It has come to accommodate those with far more dangerous ideologies. The culture of trolls and trolling is often used to attract susceptible young men and seed far-right ideology. It has become a worrying path to radicalisation.

From 'just for lulz' to violent Nazi

Ginger Gorman's *Troll Hunting* debunked many myths about the makeup and approach of internet trolls. She discovered that not all trolls work in isolation: many are part of a network of well-organised, often international, syndicates. These groups have certain insider language, distinct cultures and clear governance. They operate the way some gangs might – some liken themselves to the mafia or the yakuza. Gorman also makes clear that the term 'trolling' encompasses a range of complex and sometimes conflicting behaviours with myriad motivations – some trolls relish in getting a reaction, others are politically motivated, others still just want to spread chaos.

Gorman notes that there is an undeniable element of sexism and racism associated with trolling, with women and people of colour disproportionately the target of abuse from trolls. Most trolls are men, and a common thread is a discomfort with the way that power dynamics are shifting in contemporary society, where women and people of colour have stronger voices and are demanding equality. As journalist Van Badham puts it, 'You have generations of men who have grown up with an expectation of advantage who don't have it anymore. And that displacement in status … has made a lot of ordinary people very angry.'[3]

In 2020, the eSafety Commissioner – Australia's independent regulator for online safety – released research confirming that journalists are more likely to be targets of online abuse if they are female, LGBTQI+, Aboriginal or Torres Strait Islander, from a culturally or linguistically diverse background, or living with a disability.[4] The risk factors are magnified by 'intersectionality' – when someone possesses more than one of these characteristics. Females are more likely to experience abuse related to their appearance, threats of a sexual nature and abuse that contains misogynistic language, while those from culturally diverse backgrounds are more likely to receive abuse about their ethnicity or their cultural identity and that questions their capabilities by disparaging them with terms such as 'diversity hires'. Ultimately trolls are very aware of power dynamics, which is why they target groups or segments of the population that have traditionally been demeaned: they relish the power and hurt they can exert over these groups.

Studies have attempted to construct a psychological profile of the typical troll. The research found that trolls are likely to be male and have high psychopathy and high sadism traits.[5] Psychopathy is characterised by deceitful and callous behaviour, and a general lack of personal responsibility. This suggests that trolls have an empathy deficit. Sadism is characterised by gaining pleasure from others' suffering, regardless of whether this suffering is physical or psychological. It was the most powerful indicator for trolls or trolling behaviour. There's also an interesting interaction between sadism and self-esteem, suggesting that trolls don't troll because they have low self-esteem – they do it because the more they hurt others, the better they feel about themselves.[6]

It is unsurprising that this psychological profile is also attracted to extreme ideas and ideology. Not all trolls are extremists, but trolling is often a gateway activity for future cyberterrorists and neo-Nazis. As such, trolling is a symptom of a broken online landscape, where angry young men can become radicalised in a short space of time. The image of the Hateful Troll is no longer just of a dysfunctional, basement-dwelling loner; it may also be of an educated, articulate ideologue who uses sophisticated recruitment techniques, online propaganda and content dissemination strategies to enlist others to his cause.

Dr Kaz Ross studies neo-Nazism and far-right extremists. She has seen how online platforms radicalise 'simple trolls' and draw them into extreme and violent movements. She believes the 'great meme period' and 'meme wars' were a significant scouting opportunity for extremist recruiters. A meme is a (usually humorous) image, video or text that is shared rapidly by internet users, often with slight variations. 'Memeing' – creating and spreading memes in a humorous, ironic and often abusive way, usually as a reaction to an event – is a key part of trolling. Many think that they are just poking fun at a victim's expense, but posting specific memes can also signal to others a troll's receptivity or possible openness to more extreme beliefs. 'The thing about memeing is that there's no notion of too much,' Dr Ross tells me; the point of sharing memes is to keep pushing, keep mocking, keep having the smarter reaction, the 'last snark'. There's always a more extreme version that can be created, an 'edgier' version to share.

Dr Ross explains how the new extremist groups of today exist entirely online: 'they met online, the found each other online, without these forums they couldn't have met, and they wouldn't have been able to organise'. She points the finger specifically at Steve Bannon, former Chief Strategist and Counselor to the President under Donald Trump, for amplifying many of the hateful, racist and far-right ideas in circulation online today. She says that Breitbart News, the American far-right media network of which he was executive chairman, 'really pioneered the hate' that we see online today.

She also despairs at how many young men are spending 'thousands of hours online' – on sites such as YouTube, Discord, the chans and in gaming platforms. Often they just have content playing in the background from specific sites or let the YouTube recommendation engine serve up more of the same content. In such situations, the propaganda becomes almost subliminal. Some of these internet addicts may not be actively listening to the details but are left with a general impression of the main themes in far-right ideology – for example, that Jews are bad, gays are degenerates, white people are being replaced, the world is falling apart because of minority groups, and so on.

In other words, the current set-up of the internet is facilitating the radicalisation of many young men. The lack of government regulation allows hateful websites and bad actors to publish with impunity; insufficiently moderated social network platforms allow extremist groups to coordinate and actively recruit new members; and impressionable young men, angry at the world and with time on their hands, are led down dangerous paths. This is why is it critical that we address the infrastructure of online platforms.

Why the internet makes us rage and hate

What is it about the internet that is facilitating young men to turn from Hateful Trolls to criminals and extremists? Why is it so easy to feel angry online? And why do online stoushes (whether we are part of them or just bystanders) feel like an inevitability when logging on to certain platforms, such as Twitter?

Most digital platforms and social media networks are highly engineered. Specific decisions were made in the architecture, layout, interface and functionality of digital platforms. Many are centred on facilitating 'engagement', 'a seamlessness experience' and 'maximum time on site'.

Disembodied communication

The base word for 'communication' comes from the Latin *communicare*, which means 'to share, join or create', and the Latin noun *communis*, meaning 'community or commonness'. Its etymology is about sharing and creating between groups. Welsh cultural critic Raymond Williams said that 'society is a form of communication'. He considered it central to our collective reality: 'We talk and write ourselves into existence. We construct our world word by word and image by image, as well as brick by brick.' In fact, it's impossible for humans *not* to communicate. Paul Watzlawick, Janet Beavin Bavelas and Don D. Jackson understood that 'silence can speak volumes, as can an eye roll, a glassy stare, or simply ignoring someone'.[7]

We are often quite bad at communicating, and the many reasons why are far too complex to delve into here. But one reason why this occurs online is that the internet has helped to remove the corporeal aspect – that is, a body or identity, grounded in space and time – from our communication.

Albert Mehrabian, a professor emeritus of psychology at the University of California, developed the now-famous research study which revealed that 93 per cent of our communication is non-verbal while only 7 per cent is verbal. More specifically, communication is 55 per cent body language, 38 per cent tone of voice and 7 per cent words.[8] A raft of contemporary studies have showed the importance of non-verbal communication. Researcher Heike Jacob and her team found that non-verbal cues were the decisive factor in judging other people's emotional states. Academics Markus Koppensteiner and Greg Siegle explored the link between body movements and speech.[9] But Mehrabian's '7-38-55' rule persists because it's relatively simple to remember. It is an easy-to-understand shorthand for the idea that we generally derive a lot more meaning and context from a face-to-face interaction than we do from other, disembodied forms of communication.

When sharing the same physical space, humans are adept at picking up on cues from one another that we may miss online. We can tell if someone is uncomfortable by their eye contact, bored by their fidgeting, flirty by their smile. Communication is active and embodied, linked to a specific person doing or saying a specific thing at a specific time. Online, a lot of non-verbal information is absent. Context, cues and character are lost when you reduce communication to only the bits and bytes. Like a giant game of Telephone, we relay the wrong messages to one another continually until we are regularly misunderstanding each other. We speak all at once instead of taking turns. We respond without thinking, shout without listening.

The internet, by giving everyone the ability to comment on anything at any time, fosters the conceit that all opinions are of equal value. With no gestures or vocals to soften the delivery, we judge others harshly on their words. Commenting becomes a game in which we seek to invalidate others' views if we don't share them. In such an environment, it is easy to have knee-jerk reactions of annoyance towards others. For some, that outrage is intoxicating.

For trolls, the act of disembodying ourselves from our words seemingly creates a licence to act appallingly. Freed from physical consequences, trolls air their nastiest, most hostile views to the world because they think they can. Surely their words will simply blend into the noisy miasma of online chatter and they will not be held to account for what they said? Surely it's just a little fun? They write things to others they would never dream of saying to someone's face, where they would have to witness their victim's physical response. They offer jokes when someone is being sincere, hatred when someone is being vulnerable. This corrosive behaviour makes the online world an uncomfortable and at times unsafe space for everyone else.

Spreading outrage online

Social contagion researchers Nicholas A. Christakis and James Fowler study the science of (offline) social networks – that is, our social connections to friends, family, colleagues, acquaintances and so on. They found that any individual has an enormous capacity to influence our wider social networks with our emotions and behaviours and cause a ripple effect. At its best, this is a glorious thing: one person's generosity can spark a chain reaction of kindness.[10] It can also work in reverse, where one person's cruelty can influence others to behave poorly.

We see this same pattern reflected in our online social networks. While inspirational memes and messages can spread quickly on social media, information that makes others feel angry and outraged is also far too easy to disseminate. Atomised content – content that is split into digestible chunks and shared across a range of platforms – can lack context and nuance. Such content is prone to sparking moral outrage because readers are only being given a snippet of the whole picture. Without proper context, and especially with an inflammatory headline or caption, it becomes very easy to read the worst into what you're seeing.

Neuroscientist Molly J. Crockett describes moral outrage as a 'powerful emotion that motivates people to shame and punish wrong-doers'. It is 'triggered by stimuli that call attention to moral norm violations'. Moral outrage benefits from the network effect of social platforms, with reactions visible to different groups online in a public declaration of that person's 'virtue'. The internet also lowers the cost of moral outrage, as we are all able to participate in being outraged with just a click or a comment, unlike in the real world. Crockett notes that studies have shown that 'venting anger begets more anger.

If digital media makes it easier to express outrage, this could intensify subsequent experiences of outrage.'[11] It is therefore not only easier to become outraged but we can get caught in a cycle where we are constantly reacting to inflammatory atomised content, starting a wave of indignation that can spread to our wider social networks and soon become a tsunami.

Filter bubbles

Tech entrepreneur Eli Pariser is credited with popularising the term 'filter bubbles'. Pariser is a pioneer in online engagement, having co-founded Avaaz, an online activist network, and Upworthy, a website dedicated to positive storytelling that curates viral content. Pariser defined a filter bubble as 'your own personal universe of information that's generated by algorithms that are trying to guess what you're interested in. And increasingly online we live in these bubbles. They follow us around. They form part of the fabric of most websites that we visit.'[12] Pariser finds this troubling. 'We don't know ... who an algorithm thinks we are and therefore we don't know how it's deciding what to show us or what not to show us. And it's often not showing us a part that's the most important – we don't know what piece of the picture we're missing because by definition it's out of view,' he says. Users think they are seeing a range of content when in fact they are trapped in a filter bubble created by algorithms.

A filter bubble forms when we are constantly fed content that reinforces our pre-existing biases and preferences. As we like, click on and share content that appeals to us, algorithms take this as a signal to show more of the same content, thus creating a 'bubble' of our own biases. We stop seeing content and information that challenges us. We only see other people who are the share similar views, and they only see us.

At scale, this creates an environment of destructive tribalism. Roger McNamee, an early investor in Facebook and now one of its biggest critics, claims in his book *Zucked* that people 'stop interacting with people with whom they disagree, reinforcing the power of the bubble. They go to war against any threat to their bubble, which for some users means going to war against democracy and legal norms. They disregard expertise in favour of voices from their tribe. They refuse to accept uncomfortable facts, even ones that are incontrovertible.'[13]

While tribalism has always existed, technology has amplified it. There is an evolutionary benefit to tribalism: humans are social animals, and we seek to form cohesive groups by connecting with others. We become loyal to those groups and their ideologies. In *Connected*, Nicholas Christakis and James Fowler write about *homophily*, the 'conscious and unconscious tendency to associate with people who resemble us (the word literally means "love of being alike")': 'Whether it's Hells Angels or Jehovah's Witnesses, drug addicts or coffee drinkers, Democrats or Republicans, stamp collectors or bungee jumpers, the truth is that we seek out those people who share our interests, histories, and dreams. Birds of a feather flock together.'[14] This in itself is not a bad thing. However, it starts to become dangerous if algorithms leverage our online behaviour to filter out views that are valid but contradict our own.

Algorithms do not function in a socially responsible way. Online platforms seem to have inadvertently tapped into our weakest, basest drives for outrage and tribalism. As we navigate the internet through filter bubbles, we have started to mistake speed and detail for comprehension and expertise. We have even started to create our own filter bubbles around our beliefs, seeking out like-minded people who share them. 'If you have some hesitations about vaccinations, why look for information from doctors and scientists when you can click on articles supporting vaccination-related autism? Why believe climate change is real when it's politically more convenient for you to search for conspiracy theory pieces to back up your ignorance? Why believe that the world is round when there are thousands of groups on social media declaring that it's flat?' McNamee declares.[15]

This illusion of authority is also conducive to arguments. Life in a filter bubble makes it easy to start an interaction from an aggressive position. Once you're in an argument, it is hard to break free of the competitive desire to 'win', given that anyone can follow a public online conversation. Discussions thus become opportunities for rivalry and aggression as opposed to exchanges of information and views.

A flame war is a lengthy back-and-forth online, usually escalating to insults and profanity. McNamee describes the phenomenon:

> [S]o much of our time online is spent arguing or feeding arguments … Few of these arguments change people's minds. Because the arguments are digitally veiled and lack the clear-cut consequences of tangible confrontations, both parties can get away with devolving into snarky personal attacks and passive ambiguity – the least effective tools of human relations.[16]

Dale Carnegie, author of *How to Win Friends and Influence People in the Digital Age*, adds, 'The moment you use a medium to criticize, the subject of your criticism is compelled to defend. And when another is defensive, there is little you can say to break through the barriers he has raised. Everything you say is then filtered through skepticism, or worse, complete incredulity.'[17] Flame wars are not the same as trolling, but they are symptomatic of a growing epidemic of bad behaviour online.

Scattered minds

Nicholas G. Carr's influential 2011 book, *The Shallows: What the Internet Is Doing to Our Brains*, presents a compelling, thorough and systematic condemnation of the internet. It's harmful to our ability to learn, our very ability to think, he writes:

> The Net is, by design, an interruption system, a machine geared for dividing attention. That's not only a result of its ability to display many different kinds of media simultaneously. It's also the result of the ease with which it can be programmed to send and receive messages ... psychological research long ago proved what most of us know from experience: frequent interruptions scatter our thoughts, weaken our memory, and make us tense and anxious. The more complex the train of thought we're involved in, the greater the impairment the distractions cause.[18]

Humans are by nature seduced by the distractions of the internet as we are constantly seeking stimuli. Swedish neuroscientist Torkel Klingberg agrees that human beings 'want more information, more impressions, and more complexity' and that we tend to 'seek out situations that demand concurrent performance or situations in which [we] are overwhelmed with information'.[19] The internet returns us to a primal state of superficial attentiveness, when we regularly scanned our environment for food, shelter, danger and opportunities. Scanning is therefore natural to us, and it's a time-saver. Offline, we used to scan newspapers to get the parts of news we were most interested in. We used to browse gossip magazines for the juiciest articles and photos. The ability to scan and browse is as valid a form of cognition as deep reading and concentration. However, when scanning and skimming becomes our default way of consuming information, Carr notes, it is a worrying trend. Are we now only capable of processing and communicating in an atomised manner, and do we have trouble thinking and processing on a deeper level?

Part of the challenge is that technology companies value the speedy, superficial behaviours brought about by atomised content and disruption design. Common commercial metrics include reach (how many people have seen your content, even for three seconds), impressions (the number of times your content is displayed) and clicks (how many people have clicked on your content). This translates to consumption by as many people as possible as quickly as possible. A social feed is designed to facilitate this, only accommodating very short previews that link outwards to longer pieces. The default design of search engines is also geared towards the most amount of views and clicks. Irene Au, former head of user experience at Google, confirms that its goal is 'to get users in and out really quickly. All design decisions are based on that strategy.'[20] Google's revenue model is directly tied to how many people view pages and click links. Google Adwords are robotically optimised to present compelling, eye-catching advertising copy to grab our attention. It is commercially beneficial for Google if users click on as many things as possible, as often as possible.

Being distracted by links, ads and messages is creating a kind of mental multi-tasking that is fast becoming our new normal. There are implications for our neural biology. We have learned that our brains are malleable – neural pathways adapt depending on the mental activities we prioritise. Neurons that 'fire together, wire together'. As we spend more time scanning, skimming and browsing, our neurons rewire to make us better scanners and browsers. But Nicholas Carr declares that a kind of devolution is taking place: 'What we're experiencing is, in a metaphorical sense, a reversal of the early trajectory of civilization: we are evolving from being cultivators of personal knowledge to being hunters and gatherers in the electronic data forest.' Perhaps this is why we have become more belligerent and angrier: the current structure of the internet is making us shallower thinkers, less prone to reason and more willing to spend our hours clicking on links, arguing and trolling online.

Halting the hate

With disembodied communication removing the consequences of negative interactions, social networks and atomised content making it easy to react with outrage and share this outrage outwards, filter bubbles causing us to become more insular and tribal, and our brains being rewired away from deep thinking, it is no wonder that the Hateful Troll has become a phenomenon. While some trolls are little more than nuisances, many cause real harm. We must find a way to halt the hate.

The designs of the most popular digital platforms amplify our basest instincts and facilitate rage and hate. We can and must do what we can to resist, but most importantly, we can and must hold these Big Tech companies to account. We must demand they change their platforms, and even build alternative ones.

What can individuals do?

Seek out help

First and foremost, anyone being subjected to serious online abuse, harassment or hate speech should consider reporting it to the relevant authorities. Police are becoming savvier in tracking down online trolls in the real world; however, this cat-and-mouse game will continue as each side learns how to get the better of the other. Trolls deliberately set out to hurt others, especially those they perceive to be vulnerable. This has resulted in serious psychological harm and, in some sad cases, even death. Please treat this phenomenon seriously. If you are being targeted by a troll, don't feel you have to stay silent. Seek help and do not suffer alone.

If you think you or someone in your life might be a troll, encourage them too to seek out professional help. Some of the underlying motivations for trolling behaviour, such as anger and frustration, may be worked through with a professional counsellor – a healthier outlet for these emotions.

Understand the healthy threshold for time spent online

Common among trolls is the habit of spending an excessive amount of time online. Many trolls are young men or teenagers, and their relationship with the internet borders on addiction. Limiting screen time is a good practice for everyone, but especially for those who engage in unhealthy behaviour on the internet. The Australian Institute of Family Studies notes that for teenagers, excessive screen time can have a negative impact on self-esteem and psychosocial health. Teachers, parents and peers can all play a role in helping to teach young people how to establish healthy patterns around screen time, though ultimately the person with the most agency is the individual themselves.

A pattern of excessive screen time can start well before the teenage years. There are raging online debates about how much screen time is healthy for children – any parenting website or blog will have an opinion. The Australian Health Department gives some recommendations on its website, citing evidence that screen time for children under two years old 'may be connected with delays in language development' and suggesting that children aged two to five have less than one hour of screen time per day. It also notes that screen time has 'been shown to increase between the ages of 10 and 14, especially among boys, and recommends that, outside of schoolwork, young people aged five to seventeen have 'no more than two hours of sedentary recreational screen time per day'.[21]

Do not feed the trolls

This statement has become internet lore, but it carries a fundamental truth – trolls aim to get a reaction, so one of the best things to do is simply not give them that satisfaction. Some psychologists suggest that this does not mean ignoring them, although this is a valid tactic, but becoming 'active bystanders'. Bystanders are those who witness trolling behaviour, and active bystanders step in, call out the behaviour and publicly acknowledge that it's not okay.

Calling out bad behaviour does not mean engaging in an angry back-and-forth but simply explaining that a troll's behaviour is unacceptable. Being calm, clear and firm in your condemnation of their actions is the best approach. We should all cultivate a no-tolerance policy for bad behaviour online. Most online platforms now have reporting tools, and trolls who violate community safety standards should always be reported, so that (hopefully) the site's administrators can take appropriate action.

Stop and pause

The current structure of the internet is not conducive to thoughtful reactions, reflections and nuance, but the opposite – knee-jerk reactions, thoughtlessness and misrepresentations. It's important we realise that most headlines, captions and posts we see online are likely missing key contextual information.

It's near impossible to present a nuanced, thoughtful argument in a tweet, or even a series of tweets. The back-and-forth nature of online discussion also limits our ability to communicate our intentions and the full scope of our meaning clearly. So it's worth pausing and taking a moment to properly consider facts, context and meaning before reacting to someone else's post or comment online. The design of most online platforms deters users from taking time to pause and reflect, so it's important we try to build this in ourselves. However, ultimately the platforms need to change, too.

Reframe the narrative

Just as Carly Findlay did to great effect with her Reddit trolls, reframing the narrative can be a powerful way to fight back. Trolls thrive in the shadows, emboldened by the anonymity of online commenting in certain forums. Presenting factual, accurate information objectively may take the heat out of a troll's provocative and ultimately baseless claims. Given that trolls are out to get a reaction and so aim to agitate our emotions, resetting the tenor of the conversation and maintaining engagement only on these terms, while easier said than done, can pay dividends.

What can governments and society do?

Invest in moderation features, systems and staff

One of the thorniest issues with the contemporary internet is its scale and governance. The largest social networks prize a deregulated, hands-off approach from government. They would prefer to let users rail at one another. This is because proper moderation costs time and money.

Reddit is perhaps the mainstream platform with the largest number of moderation features available to users, including upvotes and downvotes, which sees much abusive and angry content downvoted until it disappears, and useful, interesting content upvoted. The forums are also designed to be self-contained, with each 'subreddit' or specific forum governed by moderators who set up clear rules of engagement and guidelines. Still, Reddit is far from perfect, and many trolls continue to find purchase on the platform.

Wikipedia is another example of a site with a culture of moderation and user management. It encourages user editing and management – the aim is that through multiple editors contributing to and editing the content, an agreed version is reached. While this doesn't always play out as intended, and there may be issues around the veracity of the information, Wikipedia was established with a culture of respect and civility in mind, and for the most part has been able to sustain it.

Meanwhile, the worst examples – which also happen to be the most popular digital platforms – have almost no moderation capabilities. Abuse runs rampant in certain quarters and users are left to rail against one another without much recourse. Facebook and YouTube are notorious for their underinvestment in human moderation, preferring instead to rely on AI algorithms, which regularly get things wrong. Twitter, while it has more moderation (at the moment) than Facebook and YouTube, still embodies the kind of atomised, shallow way of communicating that can give rise to arguments and abuse.

Effective online management of forums and communities are important and specialist skills. Given that most digital platforms do not invest nearly enough in moderation, often it is left to profile owners, journalists and professional community managers. Groups such as Community Managers Australia, an organisation dedicated to training others in managing, planning and building online communities, help users to enforce community standards and etiquette on platforms and deserve greater recognition and funding.

But ultimately, the costs of moderation should not be borne by users and external companies. The digital platforms and product owners need to invest in these resources themselves. To make any material difference to the rage culture of certain sections of the internet, platforms must invest significantly more in human moderation and implement robust tools that allow users to manage the civility of communication online.

Create friction in online products and platforms

A 'seamless' experience was once the sacred principle for product designers creating any online products or features. The naivety of this vision has now been proven as we see the myriad consequences of a boundary-less and unrestricted digital world.

Friction is the antithesis of seamlessness and deliberately interrupts velocity and virality. It can help limit false information, online abuse and trolling. Friction is any step, content, feature or process in an online platform or product that creates an opportunity for users to pause and consider their behaviour. This can include things like:

- providing more information about the user who posted the content, including their location, relationship to the reader and affiliations or expertise
- providing more information about the content, such as where it's been shared from, whether it's part of a larger article, and how much it has been altered from its original source

- giving users more choice on the method and levels of targeting they are subjected to
- allowing some degree of randomness in content algorithms and content curation recommendations, facilitating differing opinions and subject matter
- limiting microtargeting (using consumer data and demographics to identify and influence small groups)
- introducing more checkboxes and choice screens during the process of posting online. For example, Twitter recently trialled a choice box on the retweet button function, asking users whether they're sure they want to retweet that tweet – which resulted in about a third of users choosing not to retweet.

Building friction into online products disrupts the thoughtless cycle of reaction and counter-reaction, rage baiting and outrage, which can fuel trolling and online abuse.

Have clear and enforceable content policies

Just as tools for self-regulation and community management are important to maintain civility and respect on social media, enforcing community standards and punishing those who breach these rules must also be part of the mix. For a long time, mainstream social networks considered banning and deplatforming a last resort, anxious to avoid negative publicity around 'censorship'. But this is beginning to shift as users, victims of abuse and even government legislators are demanding Big Tech companies take accountability, with increased calls for action from campaign groups, the public and government departments like the eSafety Commission.

Studies show that deplatforming works. Trolling, abusive behaviour and spreading disinformation online must not be tolerated and trolls who engage in this should be deplatformed. Having clear standards and policies will leave no doubt about what's acceptable and what's not within any given online forum or platform.

Build digital platforms without profit-driven and extractive models

Many users recognise the harms of digital platforms but find it simply impractical to disconnect, given the impact of social media in their personal lives and workplaces. As companies such as Google and Meta come to dominate the internet in more and more ways, there are limited alternatives.

However, a small number of companies have developed successful non-profit, community-based networks explicitly designed to increase the public good. In the United States, Vermont-based Front Porch Forum is essentially an actively moderated local email list centred on local community issues and discussions. It has been carefully managed over the last twenty years (which is eons in internet time) with clear rules of engagement and active moderation. Local residents find the forum useful and engaging.

In Taiwan, digital minister Audrey Tang took inspiration from citizen hacktivists and put online collaboration at the core of governance. The official national platform, Join, has more than four million users. It harvests feedback from citizens and hosts collaborative meetings where stakeholders are asked to find solutions and form a consensus on policy and local issues. The nation also has a citizen-run platform called vTaiwan, focusing on grassroots-level engagement, which hosts debates on real-world policy.

The French government developed a messaging app called Tchap, which is used by French public officials for administrative business. Amsterdam-based PublicSpaces is a network of public broadcasters, filmmakers and the Dutch arm of Wikimedia, which came together to provide an alternative software ecosystem that serves the common interest and does not seek profit. They provide email acounts, digital profile accounts, content rating and management systems.

One of the Centre for Responsible Technology's core initiatives is The Public Square Project, which seeks to reimagine the public square and wrest it back from platforms such as Google and Facebook, which have taken over large swathes of it. The Public Square Project proposed building digital infrastructure that is publicly owned and publicly run. It is inspired by Reithian principles – John Reith established the tradition of independent public broadcasting through his work at the BBC – of an independent but publicly funded entity with a remit to 'inform, educate and entertain'. The Public Square Project imagines public broadcasters as potential hosts of this new infrastructure. With a non-profit imperative, the focus would be on community building, diversity and representation, and information sharing. Ultimately, while reforming and redesigning digital platforms is critical to a healthier online experience, we will also need to reimagine and build alternative platforms that operate on new and different models.

———

Trolling is a symptom of an online environment that has turned toxic, magnifying arguments and disagreements, radicalising angry young people and providing avenues for abuse within opaquely run and unaccountable online platforms. Stopping trolls will require not just personal vigilance but system-wide changes as well.

5

The Dating App Pest

Just one boob? pleads a text message. It's a pathetic attempt at online seduction.

Or what about this effort to make a dating profile bio timelier during a pandemic? 'Quarantine is just like my penis, they're both way too long.'

Or there's a Jekyll-to-Hyde transformation when the user doesn't get a response: *Hey :)* is followed by *bitch whore* within minutes.

These messages are from Straight White Boys Texting, a website that curates examples of the absurd, regularly uninvited online dating app messages from 'straight white boys' – a generalisation, of course, more a mindset than an actual demographic, but illustrative of the modern-day Romeos who embody the perils of contemporary dating and relationships.

For anyone under thirty-five, it may be surprising, even quaint, that online dating used to have an air of the ridiculous. Anyone who found love through the internet would be subjected to bad jokes about 'Russian brides' or 'Filipina mail orders'. Even recently, prospective love interests from Tinder would be disparaged as 'Tinderellas' or 'Tinderfellas'.

The origins of online dating are actually in the 1960s, when computers first emerged. Dating services promised to put new, efficient and rational computing power to task on helping the loveless find their soulmates. As *The Atlantic* described it:

> In the 1960s, what was known as 'computer dating' involved no internet and often few to no visuals. People submitted their vital stats along with questionnaires by mail. Not e-mail, of course, but old-fashioned, stamp-licking mail. No instant gratification followed. People waited patiently for days, weeks, and months as companies processed their answers on intelligence, attractiveness, quirks, and preferences, and would perhaps find them matches ... the hope for true love. The questionnaire model dated back to the Scientific Marriage Foundation in 1957 and flourished throughout the '60s and '70s.[1]

It wasn't until three decades later, in the 1990s, that personal computers became a common sight in homes. The internet also connected us globally. Match.com was one of the services that launched in the 1990s, and it promised something none of the others did: real-time matching.

Over time, our relationship with computers and the internet started to change. We got comfortable using email for work, browsing the web to research and buy things, and using chat and instant messaging to communicate. As we used the internet and digital communication for more everyday tasks, we gradually started to get more comfortable using it for dating as well. By 2005, Match.com had 40 million registered users. According to a University of Chicago study by led psychologist John Cacioppo, 'more than one third of those married between 2005 and 2012 met on-line'. Online dating was the main way people met their spouses – more met online than at work, through friends and at school combined.[2] Cacioppo's findings were so shocking that many questioned their validity; some argued that the research was biased because it was commissioned by an online dating company. But the findings were largely consistent with those of Stanford University sociologist Michael Rosenfeld. His survey, 'How couples meet and stay together', is a nationally representative study of 4000 Americans that paints a similar picture.

This trend would continue to grow with the launch of online dating apps. Tinder is the market leader today. Two University of California undergraduates, Sean Rad and Justin Mateen, wanted to create an online dating experience that felt more like a game, something easy and fun. As of January 2022, there were approximately 75 million people using Tinder every month all over the world, across 190 countries and in forty languages. Approximately 60 billion matches have been recorded, with people spending an average of thirty-five minutes a day swiping.[3]

Other popular apps include Bumble, where women are empowered to make the first contact, and Hinge, an attempt at something slightly less superficial than the swipe mentality of Tinder. For gay men there's Grindr, Scruff and Hornet. For gay women there's Her and Fem. There's JSwap for Jewish people, Christian Mingle for Christians, Single Muslim for Muslims. Patrio is for conservatives who only want to date other conservatives, Hater matches people based on what they don't like, Awake helps you find your fellow conspiracy theorists and Bro is for bromances. There is a long menu of options to choose from, catering to a diverse range of tastes and goals.

Online dating has gone from taboo to become the single largest source of romantic partners. 'Today, if you own a smartphone, you're carrying a 24/7 singles bar in your pocket,' declares Aziz Ansari in his book *Modern Romance*.[4] For some, online dating apps are more than a convenience – they're critical. Mark, thirty-two, says, 'I wouldn't have a dating life if I wasn't online … girls my age all use them.' He even declares that the once-reliable bar hookup is now the exception rather than the rule. 'Girls act weird if you try and talk to them in a bar [without first having met online]. They just don't respond to you.' Sarah, twenty-eight, validates this perception. 'I'm a little bit suspicious if you come up to me in a bar and I think you're trying to get me interested, especially if I don't see you online.'

For some, social media is more important than dating apps. Pete, thirty-seven, finds dates on Instagram and Facebook. 'I'm on Grindr and Scruff, but I still meet a lot of people on Instagram and Facebook.' After all, Facebook came to life in nineteen-year-old Mark Zuckerberg's Harvard University dorm room and was developed to rate the attractiveness of his fellow students. You could argue that one of the largest technology platforms today was initially concerned with online dating.

It's not just singles in their twenties and thirties connecting online, either. Singles in their fifties and sixties, who find themselves on the other side of a divorce, separation or the loss of the partner, are also using dating apps, albeit not necessarily Tinder. 'Tinder seems too aggressive,' says Carolina, fifty-seven. She stopped using some online dating services because there wasn't a large-enough pool of people her age, but eventually found Bumble. For Carolina, there is a real opportunity for the online dating services to better cater for her age group. 'This is a big business and they are missing out,' she says.

In fact, while young straight people have benefited most from online dating, the change is even more dramatic for what Rosenfield dubs 'thin markets', notably 'people interested in same-sex relationships, but increasingly older and middle-aged straight people too. The reason is pretty obvious: the smaller the pool of potential romantic partners, the lower the odds of finding romance face-to-face, whether through friends, in schools or in public places.' Rosenfield's research shows that online dating is 'dramatically more common among same-sex couples than any way of meeting has ever been for heterosexual or same-sex couples in the past. And recent trends suggest that as more older people go online, internet dating will start to dominate their world too.'[5]

The internet and online dating apps are key ingredients in our lives, from young to old, straight to queer, and across countries. So are we all dating app pests now? How have we changed as a result? And how do we draw the line between productive use of dating apps and problematic or even harmful use?

Online dating – friend or foe?

Kay is in her mid-thirties and lives in Brisbane. A creative who works in theatre and music, she is used to meeting interesting people through her profession, including when travelling interstate and abroad. Because of this, she only has need of dating apps if she wants to 'hook up with someone', usually while travelling. She admits that she began using dating apps casually, 'like a game', and did not take them very seriously. This 'game' would even involve plugging her phone into a friend's television during a party and having public swipings for the party to participate in. It was a form of entertainment for her and her friends.

But during lockdown, she found she had a lot of time on her hands and was jarred by the isolation, in contrast with her usually lively and very social life. It was during this period that she 'began using dating apps seriously'. This meant that she was determined 'to find a man' (and not just a random hookup). Starting off on Tinder, she was very quickly turned off by the cut-throat nature of the app. 'Men would get straight to the [hookup] part', asking for photos straight away and assuming sex would follow. 'They didn't even know my name and they would just keep asking for pics.' Although this was primarily how she had used Tinder in the past, it was jarring to her now that she was looking to develop a more serious relationship. She moved on to Bumble.

'Bumble was a little better,' she says, but she was surprised by how many men she encountered who simply needed someone to talk to. 'I felt like a therapist. Men on Bumble were just looking for someone to nurture them.'

After dozens of failed encounters, it seemed like a hopeless endeavour. While her Bumble experiences gave rise to lots of comedic anecdotes that her friends enjoyed, online dating required time and investment. It took up almost all her spare hours.

But, still determined, she finally landed on Hinge, after searching for 'best online dating apps'. Hinge had a few more success stories, and there seemed to be actual functioning men on the platform. It was the only app where she felt she could meet the type of man she could see herself being with. After dozens of matches, hundreds of conversations and a serious vetting process, there were only three men she finally met.

One was a man of a similar age to her, with similar tastes in music and with whom she could have a decent conversation. After a very successful first date (or so she thought), he abruptly ended the interaction by declaring that was 'just no spark' between them.

She had instant chemistry with the next man: great banter and, again, similar tastes in music. He lived in Melbourne, which in retrospect should have been a red flag, given she was in Brisbane. But he said he travelled to Brisbane for work regularly, so meeting up wasn't an issue. After many days of good conversation, she was excited to finally meet him. 'It would've been about 9.00 am and we were due to go have breakfast. He literally walked out of [his friend's place, where he was staying] with three beers in his hands: one he was finishing, one he was cracking open, and one for the road.' After bad experiences with an alcoholic partner a few years earlier, this was the worst possible first impression he could have given Kay. Interestingly, they stayed in touch, even though the date was a bust. They became friends and she now sees him as 'more of an older brother'. He later revealed that his appearance on their date was orchestrated 'to see how she would react'. The idea was that if she was 'cool with it', she could clearly accept the worst he had to offer and was worthy of a potential relationship.

The last was a man who only seemed interested in hooking up and would periodically disappear or 'ghost' her. They had a connection when they met – there was good chemistry and great sex. But once that brief period was over, he wouldn't contact her or reply to any of her messages. She would eventually think that was it, only to hear from him again weeks later, and the cycle would repeat. Finally, after months of this, she confronted him about it. He said he was really introverted, and it took all his social energy to muster up the charisma, energy and enthusiasm for those brief but intensely pleasurable sessions, after which he would need to recharge in his own company again. Because of this energy deficit, he felt he could not sustain a long-term adult romantic relationship.

Kay is surprisingly gracious when recalling these examples. Out of dozens and dozens of interactions, she could only find three encounters that weren't completely disastrous. Even then, one of those men dismissed her, another thought he had to act appallingly to 'test' her resolve and a third could not maintain enough social energy for anything more than a fleeting hookup.

These dire situations are what Australian women often face today when online dating. But for Kay, there is something larger at play. She feels that Australian men, in general, are very dysfunctional. 'It showed me how so many men are just sad, and that we [society] are not ready for them to be this vulnerable. They don't know how to deal with it, and we don't know how to engage with it.' So the poor women who encounter them on dating apps bear the brunt.

Ben is a gay man in his thirties living in Sydney. Ben's dating app usage varies: some days he'll check an app intensely for hours; other days he won't look at it at all. On average, he thinks, he spends about fifteen to twenty hours a week on apps such as Grindr, Scruff, Hinge, Tinder and Squirt. There is a clear distinction between Grindr, Scruff and Squirt, which are primarily about sex, and Tinder and Hinge, which are more for dating. He mostly spends time on the hookup apps.

While he acknowledges that the apps can be successful in getting him dates and hookups, he says the time and energy he spends on them is 'frustrating'. There are clear distinctions in behaviour on the apps compared to at a bar. The apps are 'brutal … you get ignored … a lot of the time you have to pay for certain features'. He describes the work involved in 'wading through all the profiles, messaging people … it's a numbers game. You have to message a lot of people to get the result you want.' Much is lost through online communication – context, body language and other non-verbal communication cues. Aside from Hinge, which has a feature where you can upload a clip of your voice answering questions, he believes all the apps are generally 'dehumanising'. He also calls them 'cut-throat' and says 'it's almost like you need an instruction manual before using them'. The lack of accountability or etiquette, and the sense that there are no minimum standards of respectful behaviour, causes many users to act very badly.

Ben says several of his friends and other men he has spoken to share the view that the apps can be 'very bad for your self-esteem and your sense of self-worth'. He declares, 'The consensus is that everyone hates the apps, but it's the best thing we have right now.' The pandemic has proven challenging, given many bars and nightclubs have had restrictions placed on them. The apps are 'a massive time sink' and 'generally not a great experience' but it's hard to avoid using them when 'everyone is on there'. He does wish 'there was another way' to meet people.

―――――――

Kay and Ben are mostly on the receiving end of bad behaviour on dating apps, and rare is the person who would admit to dishing it out. But we know they're around. Mostly, they are various sorts of addicts, trapped by the gamification of dating apps and the rush of dopamine at the possibility of every match, message and potential hookup.

Therapist and relationship counsellor Lucy Cavendish describes a certain personality that is addicted to dating. Dating apps have facilitated those who love to flirt obsessively and message outrageously but never follow through on a meeting, or who go on dates with no genuine intent to find a meaningful connection, or serial daters who only want to tick a box so they can move on to the next. She says, 'It makes me wonder if we have become a nation of prospectors – dating endlessly in the certainty the next one will be The One, but in reality wasting hours of our lives with little to show for it.'[6]

There are those who are caught up in swiping endlessly even if they know it's unhealthy. 'Swiping takes so little thought, which is a big part of these kinds of addictive behaviours,' says Ohio State University researcher Kathryn Coduto.[7] Coduto's research revealed that people who are lonely and socially anxious are more likely to have unhealthy swiping behaviours. She found that such individuals can come to depend on dating apps, even if it interrupts regular responsibilities, such as school or work. The idea of meeting face-to-face becomes intimidating, so they restrict their behaviours to swiping and messaging online, which gives them an illusion of control and comfort.

Then there are serial adulterers – people who are married or in committed relationships who continue to look for hookups. Both Kay and Ben encountered many of them. Ben even hooked up with one on a regular basis.

Behaviours around online dating, relationships, love and sex are so varied, just as in the offline world. But there are some technologically and digitally driven characteristics of online apps that may help to create the Dating App Pest. It is mostly to do with the features in apps that have come to facilitate and sometimes complicate our most intimate relationships. Something as subjective as sex, or as private as a relationship, now often takes place through gamified online technology. How could there not be issues?

Why online dating reflects our troubled relationship with the internet

In many ways, online dating is a microcosm of what is happening more broadly online. As we try to navigate very human emotions and relationships through a digitally mediated environment, we encounter a host of complications.

The gamification lure

The design of many digital products fosters addiction. Dating apps are a prime example of addictive products. The founders of Tinder built the app with game mechanics in mind. The easy-to-use interface – which includes features such as swiping and tapping, progressive rewards, chimes and notifications, and microtransactions to 'unlock' extra features – is designed to hook users and make them stay. The dopamine hit gained from every reaction, message and match, and the seemingly endless menu of individuals to match with, has similarities with online gaming.

The central feature of the dating app, swiping, is powerful and habit-forming. It gives the feeling of unlimited options and the illusion of 'progress'. Swiping through profiles produces a false sense of productivity – it deludes the user into thinking that they're doing something meaningful with their time and getting closer to finding that 'perfect match' when in fact they're just wasting hours.

Even message interactions feel more like a game than real comm-unication on dating apps, with flirtations accompanied by emoticons and text abbreviations, and reactions reduced to likes and heart emojis. Plus there is always the option to simply stop interacting, taking the pressure off in terms of commitment. This reduction of social interactions that ought to be nuanced, complex and sensitive has resulted in online dating becoming, for some, an endlessly addictive game without end.

Fake profiles or fake people?

If there was ever a time to care about your online image, it is when you are searching for a date. Whether it's an app or an online questionnaire, every piece of information will be judged by your prospective viewer. Users have different approaches and tactics, all in the hope of presenting their best self online. What's the most flattering photo to use? How to capture your personality in a couple of lines? What are the best qualities to list about yourself?

On apps such as Tinder, which prioritise visuals over text, the profile photo is virtually the only information prospective matches have to go on. In *Modern Romance*, Aziz Ansari catalogues the various types of images people use on their online dating profiles. There's the selfie from above, which gives a leaner cast to your face due to the high angle; the photo with a pet, showing you're an animal lover, with the added hope that some of the animal's cuteness will transfer to you; and the partier pose, with drink in hand or occupied in some act of revelry, showing you know how to have a good time. Then there's the pensive, arty picture; the beautiful-scenery-in-the-background portrait; the casual shot that casually shows your best side; the hiding-between-attractive-friends approach, showing that good-looking people consider you part of their circle; and the strategic less-attractive-friend photo, where you pose with someone less attractive than you so you seem more attractive in context. And, of course, there are 'thirst traps', designed to up the sexual ante, showing well-angled muscles, topless torsos, abs, bikinis, long legs, ample cleavage. Ansari discovered that, for women, the most successful profile pictures tend to show most of the face and the top half of the body, with the subject looking at the camera. For men, it helps not to look straight at the camera but to gaze to the side or away into the distance. For both sexes, it's a winner if you're doing something novel, such as diving, riding a motorbike on an exotic holiday or engaged in some sort of interesting hobby – this works as a conversation starter.

The presentation of the self online is a curious thing. Portraits and images shared on dating apps and websites range from the casual to the downright explicit. Men are especial culprits when it comes to posting unwelcome images, such as the notorious 'dick pic'. Among gay men it's even more common, as messages not infrequently jump straight from *hello* to a flash of genitalia. This encourages a virtual 'cut to the chase', encouraging users to make an honest, if brutal, judgement based on appearances.

Online, people are exposed to more potential partners in any one session than they would be offline. There are both pros and cons to this. Users may encounter a wider and potentially more diverse range of matches. They are not restricted to only seeing individuals who are part of their offline circles and groups. However, this variety can cause some to develop an 'assessment mindset'. A team of psychologists led by Eli J. Finkel at Northwestern University conducted a detailed study of online dating through a psychological science lens and found that 'side-by-side browsing' causes users 'to commoditize potential partners'. Furthermore, 'many sites provide users with very large numbers of profiles, causing them to use time-efficient but minimally thoughtful strategies for choosing among them and potentially reducing their willingness to commit to any one partner'.[8] In a competitive marketplace, our online depictions become less-than-authentic representations of our true selves as we strive to stand out, and our relationships start to become transactional.

Because our online identities are mutable and we reconfigure them regularly to suit our purposes, dating apps heighten the potential for deception, misinterpretation or fiction. Yaniv 'Nev' Schulman catapulted to fame when the documentary *Catfish* was shown at the 2010 Sundance Film Festival. Schulman's story came as online dating was beginning to grow in significance and it coined a term used widely today. According to the Urban Dictionary, a catfish is 'someone who pretends to be someone they're not, using Facebook or other social media to create false identities, particularly to pursue deceptive online romances'. In the film, Schulman forms a relationship with an eight-year-old girl on Facebook when she sends him a drawing based on one of his photographs. He becomes drawn into her family circle and develops an online relationship with her older sister, Megan. The two exchange thousands of romantic messages before Schulman embarks on a road trip to meet her and discovers that Megan is not real – he is being 'catfished' by a Michigan housewife named Angela, who has created a series of imaginary profiles.

Schulman is an open critic of Facebook for twisting our idea of relationships and 'hijacking the word "friend"'. Schulman declares that being someone's friend 'used to mean something':

> Someone didn't ask to be your friend. They just became your friend because you spent time with them and showed them that you cared. They were your friend because they were present in your life, active in your happiness and supportive of your ambitions. They were accountable to you. But then Facebook came along and decided that all that's required of someone to be your friend is a mere click of a mouse. Instead of having shared life experiences with you as part of a balanced exchange of give and take, now

your 'friends' simply consume your photos and status updates. They are witnesses to your life, not participants in it. Your life online is just another content stream that distracts and entertains the people you are 'friends' with, and your identity is like another channel for people to flip through, admire, or judge.[9]

Schulman perhaps has reason to be bitter following his very public duping, although he has since developed the documentary into a reality television series, now up to its eighth season. *Catfish: The TV Show* is strangely compelling. The catfishing is in most cases merely the beginning of the story. The situations vary but the show displays a raw humanity, showcasing our collective need to love and be loved. When the catfish stories end well (a minority of cases), it can be moving. For various reasons, whether low self-esteem, issues around their sexuality or plain misfortune, catfish develop profiles based on the people they wished they were or hoped to be. In one episode, a woman catfish wanted to come clean to her online suitor. It turns out the person she'd been speaking with was also a catfish and not a cis man but a transgendered one, on the way to transitioning. The confrontation was emotional, but ultimately they chose to forgive each other's deceptions and celebrate the genuine emotional connection they had forged online.

Online, our desire to present our best selves is intensified as we seek our life partners, soulmates or just our next hookup. The plethora of potential partners to choose from on online dating apps can cause us to act in ways that are not necessarily good for us. We filter and curate every aspect of our profiles. Sometimes we even pretend a little – or a lot. But ultimately, we are simply seeking ways to love and be loved, to be celebrated for who we are and who we could be.

The tyranny of texting

Texting and messaging, and online dating overall, suffer from the atomisation phenomenon: a lack of context and other cues from non-verbal communication can lead to miscommunication and misunderstanding. The study led by Eli J. Finkel notes, 'The absence of face-to-face social cues may lead communicators to fill in the gaps in often inaccurate ways – for example, overly optimistic or overly particular views of the message sender, which can create expectations that are not confirmed when people subsequently meet face-to-face.'[10] One side effect is the anxiety that waiting for a reply can cause.

Most of us have experienced the powerful reactions provoked by the ellipsis icon, meaning someone is typing a reply but is taking a while to do so; in some cases, they won't reply at all. 'Being left on read' – meaning someone has seen your message but has yet to reply – can also be hard to deal with. 'Texting is a medium that conditions our minds in a distinctive way, and we expect our exchanges to work differently with messages than they do with phone calls … Texting has habituated us to receiving a much quicker response … When we don't get the quick response, our minds freak out,' write Aziz Ansari and sociologist Eric Klinenberg. MIT anthropologist Natasha Schüll draws an analogy between slot machines and texting: both engender the expectation of a quick reply. 'When you're texting with someone you're attracted to, someone you don't really know yet, it's like playing a slot machine: there's a lot of uncertainty, anticipation and anxiety. Your whole system is primed to receive a message back.'[11] The anticipation and the limited knowledge of the sender can cause great stress and anxiety in the hopeful.

This lack of direct contact can have other implications as well. One of the great challenges of the online world is that we are simultaneously near but far, intimate but removed. Because we are not in the same room with our interlocutor, we must overcommunicate our intentions. We need to adopt a kind of 'hyperpersonal' mode of communication, filtering our desires through texts, emojis and photographs, as psychology professor Joseph Walther and psychologist Monica T. Whitty observe.[12]

Even when there's the ability to see one another, digital communication is not quite the same as face-to-face. In *The App Generation: How Today's Youth Navigate Identity, Intimacy, and Imagination in a Digital World*, co-author Katie Davies, an associate professor at the University of Washington Information School, studies the relationship teenagers have with their phones, including her younger sister, Molly:

> Facetime (Apple's answer to Skype) can also be used to illustrate the ease of failing into a transactional rather than transformational interpersonal exchange online. When Katie and Molly first talked remotely using Facetime, the first thing Katie noticed was that genuine eye contact is impossible. If you want the other person to feel like you're looking them in the eyes, then you have to look into the camera, not their eyes. In other words, to create the illusion of eye contact one must actively avoid it. Something else that Katie noticed instantly was her own image in the corner of the screen. She found it hard not to glance at it periodically, which turned her attention away from Molly and onto herself. Apparently, Molly was equally, if not more so, enticed.[13]

Atomisation can cause filter bubbles and tribalism, as noted in the Hateful Troll chapter. This can extend to dating as well. When algorithms select only certain types of people that match a user's criteria, the user could be exposed to a narrow funnel of individuals, even though in theory online dating allows for more diverse choices. The Finkel study declares that 'although users almost universally think of online dating as expanding their field of eligible options, it may actually be shrinking crucial aspects of the diversity of that field'. Online dating and atomisation may be narrowing not only the pool of potential dates but also the types of interactions and developments that can occur when we date people who are different from us. 'Partners often help each other develop new skills and perspectives by exposing each other to activities and viewpoints … To the extent that the pool of eligible provided by an internet matching site is less diverse (ethnically, attitudinally, or in any other respect relevant to its algorithm) than the pool of eligible options encountered in ordinary activity, then we would expect less self-expansion of this sort to occur.'[14]

Whether you use online dating apps for inspiration or perspiration, they are designed to facilitate other forms of communication, not replace them.

Privacy and intimacy in a virtual world

Smartphones are funny things. Because we own them and carry them around with us, they come to feel like our own little private boxes. They keep our contacts, mail, games, apps, social media – they contain our virtual selves. They probably know more about us than our partners and friends do. They keep our confidences and our secrets.

We've become so intimate with our devices that it's not such a stretch to imagine, perhaps, being in love with them. The 2014 Spike Jonze movie *Her* was set in a techno-utopian world where AI smart assistants manage our lives. The protagonist falls in love and starts a relationship with his personal device, which is an extremely advanced version of Siri or Alexa (and which speaks in the sultry voice of Scarlett Johansson).

It seems silly, but it's not hard to see why it could be plausible for some. As we live our lives in tandem with our devices, we grow more and more connected to them. Even when all evidence points us to the contrary, we still use our devices to share our most confidential information. This is part of the 'privacy paradox' – we claim to care about our privacy but we don't protect our information online. Susan B. Barnes, a professor at the Rochester Institute of Technology, revealed that teens, often the most savvy users of technology, were avidly sharing information online even when they knew what they were sharing may expose them to risk:

> It's an interesting shift because so often in the real world, many teens are self-conscious and tend to seek privacy. But online, something else happens – their behaviour changes. Even teenagers who are well versed in the dangers and have read stories of identity theft, sextortion, cyberbullying, cybercrimes, and worse continue to share as though there is no risk.

Rochester found that privacy is a 'generational construct': 'It means one thing to baby boomers, something else to millennials, and a completely different thing to today's teenagers.'[15] Mostly this has to do with perceived levels of acceptable privacy as it relates to technology.

This desire to share online is not without an upside. Interestingly, in societies where privacy is most valued, dating apps and websites can enable valuable disclosures. In some parts of the world, they are helping young people in repressive societies find love. In Qatar, for example, casual dating is prohibited but the internet is allowing young people to connect, as Aziz Ansari and Eric Klinenberg record in *Modern Romance*:

… socializing with the opposite sex in public is not allowed, so Qataris are using the internet to organise small private parties in hotel rooms. One of the young women we met told us that hotels are a big part of Qatari culture, because that's where you find bars and restaurants, and these days it's not uncommon to receive a group message that tells people who know another to meet in a certain room. Once they arrive at the hotel lobby, the cover provided by the females' burkas allows them to wander in anonymously and go wherever they need to go. By blending something old, the burka, with something new, the Internet, Qatari youth have created their own novel way to connect.[16]

But for those in more liberal societies, we are often giving away large amounts of intimate detail to the companies that run dating apps and websites without due consideration of the risks. In 2017, *Guardian* journalist Judith Duportail asked Tinder to release all her personal data for a piece she was writing about online privacy. She had been a member since 2013. Tinder sent her 800 pages worth of her user activity. It included thousands of messages of her hopes, fears, sexual preferences and deepest secrets. 'Tinder knows me so well. It knows the real, inglorious version of me who copy-pasted the same joke to match 567, 568 and 569; who exchanged compulsively with 16 different people simultaneously one New Year's Day, and then ghosted 16 of them.' It also knew where she had been each time she logged on, stretching back years. And it had recorded 'secondary implicit disclosed information' about how she used the app. Secondary implicit disclosed information is information about how a user engages with the app. For Tinder, it can include data such as 'the percentage of white men, black men, Asian men you have matched; which kinds of people are interested in you; which words you use the most; how much time people spend on your picture before swiping you,' Alessandro Acquisti, professor of information technology at Carnegie Mellon University, told Duportail. At scale, patterns and trends in behaviour can be mapped and used to guide future product developments.

Many of us make unconscious disclosures of this kind without realising we are doing so. We are giving away enough information about ourselves that technology companies can build very specific profiles of us and can even predict our tastes and interests. When it comes to online dating, privacy is an illusion – instead, we are broadcasting our innermost thoughts, fantasies and secrets to the boardrooms of technology companies worldwide.

Finding love with or without screens

As if dating, sex and relationships aren't complicated enough, we have added a digital layer with apps and websites in which finding a partner becomes a game of roulette. We judge one another on the most superficial of measures. Our fragile selves are held to the not-so-gentle bosom of the internet, as we whisper our insecurities, secrets and hopes into the ear of tech moguls. With a series of dating sites, each with its own subculture that rewards and punishes different types of behaviour, hosted in a poorly regulated internet landscape, the virtual environment is ripe for miscommunication, misunderstanding and potential heartache. Online dating is not designed for the faint of heart.

Online dating does demonstrate, though, how our virtual and our physical worlds have become so closely interlinked in our lives that they can never be disentangled. Dating apps and websites play a crucial role in allowing people to meet and engage in (relative) safety and comfort. But ultimately, the virtual interaction must become a real-world interaction if a meaningful and healthy relationship is to develop. Many people use online dating apps successfully as an aid to their offline lives, and they delete these apps once they've found a long-term romantic partner. A more closely managed and careful experience with dating apps and websites can aid us to move seamlessly between the virtual and the physical worlds. The high-stakes pursuit of love requires the kind of approach we should be applying in all our virtual interactions.

What can individuals do?

Treat technology as a wingperson

For some, online dating has meant a new world of choice, convenience and customised connection, allowing for more dates with more interesting people. For others, it means anxiety, paranoia, unwelcome interactions and an invasion of privacy in the hope of finding that special person. For most users, it is a mix of both. This amalgam of inspiration and confusion is not surprising. When two people connect online, just as in the real world, they each bring their emotional baggage, individual personalities and unique histories, and the process of forming a relationship is about negotiating their way through this. Online dating is messy because, well, humans are messy. All the anxiety and hilarity that arises from online dating is because we sometimes forget that there is a person on the other end receiving our advances, worrying about their own desirability and suffering from the griefs of their past relationships.

Different people use online dating profiles in different ways. Some have very specific rules, while others rely on serendipity. Some approach a session on Tinder with a military precision; others are more casual, browsing idly with friends or sometimes even as a party game. But because we're all people, we all (or almost all) crave offline interaction. Online technology, and particularly online dating services, should be used to facilitate and develop offline connections. 'Ultimately, we find that the quality of our relationships in this app era depends on whether we use our apps to bypass the discomforts of relating to others or as some risky entry points to the forging of sustained, meaningful interactions,' declare psychologists Howard Gardner and Katie Davis. Eli J. Finkel and his team back up this view: 'Online dating functions best to the degree that it introduces people to potential partners they would have been unlikely to encounter otherwise and facilitates a rapid transition to face-to-face interaction, where the two people can get a clearer sense of their romantic potential.'[17] In other words, dating apps and websites are a means of enhancing and developing relationships, not a substitute for them.

It is wise to remember that while a dating app can be your best friend, your cheerleader, your wingperson, helping you gain useful information about someone you like and make the first move, it does not conduct a relationship for you. And you will never be able to fully connect with someone and build a meaningful relationship unless you disconnect from the technology and take things offline.

Use dating apps and websites meaningfully

Limitless options are actually not good for the human brain. Too much choice can be overwhelming; we simply cannot cope with the cognitive overload. The well-known 'jam study', conducted by academics at Stanford and Columbia universities, found that shoppers are more likely to buy a jar of jam if there are about six options to choose from, rather than twenty-four or thirty. If a person is presented with too many choices, they are actually *less likely* to buy anything.[18]

The 'swipe mentality', which reduces potential partners to menu options, may create a false sense of progress, with the quantity of potential matches making it seem like you've got closer to meeting the right person for you, but in fact you have not. Algorithms may be dictating who you see online, cognitive overload may mean you are overlooking good matches and your efficiency may have been achieved because you have made limited effort with each potential partner. Endlessly scrolling and swiping may limit your chances rather than increase them.

If you are online dating to find a long-term partner, creating restrictions on and being mindful about your usage of apps will help to foster more considered interactions with others and therefore increase your chances of forming a meaningful connection. Make sure that you keep questioning yourself about whether you're using the app to find someone special or simply getting caught in a swipe loop. Where the app allows, lessen the impact of the gamified and addictive features by setting your own parameters about who you see online and when.

Treat others as you would like to be treated

Many people hide behind a screen and think a lack of physical contact gives them the right to behave badly. It's simple: there is a real person on the other end of your message. The username you ghosted, the chat you forgot about, the message you didn't respond to, the picture you rejected, the greeting you blocked – it has an impact on someone's emotions.

Just as most of us wouldn't flash our privates to a stranger in the physical world, abruptly walk away from a conversation or ignore someone who is trying to talk to us because we don't find them attractive, we shouldn't practise those behaviours online. Mutual respect, consideration and basic courtesy can go a long way in the digital world. The challenge can sometimes be that we lack the social cues, shared conventions of etiquette and conversational circuit-breakers online that we rely on in the physical world. If you think others may be finding your advances unwelcome or even aggressive, think about how you might behave towards them if you met them in a real-world setting and aim to conduct yourself in the same manner.

What can governments and society do?

Create a culture of safety in online dating apps

If we accept that dating apps are part of modern life, it only makes sense that we would want to make them safer. Complaints about a lack of safety were common to many individuals I interviewed for this chapter, both men and women. It is essential that technology companies and government ensure that some basic standards of safety exist on all dating apps and websites. There should be a no-tolerance policy and a clear reporting mechanism for any predatory, harmful or abusive behaviour. The eSafety Commissioner is an important channel in which users can report bullying and abusive behaviour occurring anywhere on the internet, including in an online dating context.

However, the commissioner's limited scope means it often must focus on behaviour at the more extreme end of the spectrum. There is more that can be done around everyday issues, such as a lack of civility on dating apps. Many of my interviewees felt that dating apps are 'brutal'. The technology companies developing these products should ensure they have clear policies against discrimination. More so, they should build in safety features – including keyword filtering and banning, 'strike' policies to deter repeat offenders and software that limits any discrimination based on race, gender or sexual orientation.

Develop minimum standards of care for dating apps and websites

Government can play a role by developing a regulatory framework that outlines minimum standards of care for users of dating apps and websites, as well as for other internet sites. Such a framework would mean that technology companies would be forced to comply in implementing safety and quality features across their products. Many countries, including Australia, are considering or in the process of developing such regulatory frameworks – they cannot come soon enough.

Some people I spoke to complained of giving feedback to dating apps and websites about product improvements and receiving no response or seeing no change. Legislative standards could be designed to address key concerns that users have about safety on dating apps and websites. This could cover extreme behaviour such as cyberbullying, harassment and violence, but also the overall experience of dating apps and websites.

Reduce gamification and addictive features

Many dating apps have taken lessons from the online gaming world and built gamification features and addictive elements into their products. Any minimum standard of care developed for dating apps and websites should include rules around design principles that reduce the potential for addictive behaviours. There should be circuit-breaker options that force a user to take breaks. Building friction into online products, as we saw in the previous chapter, also creates an opportunity for users to pause and consider their behaviour.

The eSafety Commissioner promotes Safety by Design, which 'puts user safety and rights at the centre of the design and development of online products and services':

> Rather than retrofitting safeguards after an issue has occurred, Safety by Design focuses on the ways technology companies can minimise online threats by anticipating, detecting and eliminating online harms before they occur. This proactive and preventative approach focuses on embedding safety into the culture and leadership of an organisation. It emphasises accountability and aims to foster more positive, civil and rewarding online experiences for everyone.[19]

The designers of dating apps and websites can show leadership by committing to ensuring safe, well-managed, engaging spaces for their users to meet online.

As the boundaries between offline and online become less rigid, more of us are initiating our most intimate and personal relationships through screens. Online dating can be made safer and more enjoyable for all if we look out for each other – and ensure that the companies which profit from our sexual and romantic activity look out for us too.

6

The Screen Addict

I clock up about seven hours of screen time on average per day. This is just on my phone. I get an average of six to seven hours of sleep a night. Add in my eight work hours on an average weekday – which is largely spent online, given my work is internet-related – and I spend practically every waking hour I have on the web.

According to my screen diagnostics, as soon as I wake up I reach for my phone and check Instagram, then Notes (apparently I write a lot of notes to myself). I spend the most time on a mobile game called *Shop Titans* – an app where you are a merchant in a fantasy land selling goods such as enchanted swords and magic armour within a medieval village. Following this, I am once again writing notes to myself, then browsing using Safari. I spend an awful lot of time on Instagram and Twitter during the day as well.

I've never really seen this as a problem. I don't think it's disrupted my life in a material way. But should I?

I am also a casual gamer. When I'm not playing mobile games, I like to play role-playing games on my Xbox. I've been a gamer since I was a child, so my nonchalance about what many might consider excessive screen time has had a long gestation.

Gamers often get a bad rap. For most, the term brings to mind clichés of a socially inept teenage boy, oozing pimples and with Coke-bottle glasses. I have experienced these negative perceptions around gaming for many years. When you say you enjoy playing online games as an adult, you are often met with bemusement or mockery. But gaming can teach us a lot about our experience online, because the contemporary internet takes many of its most engaging features from the world of games.

From avatars to incentives, gaming was one of the first industries to capitalise on the convenience of the internet. Mobile-phone gaming through apps has seen participation and interest in gaming spike across all demographics. Now that most of us have smartphones, we are all pretty much gamers.

Market research company eMarketer declared in 2021 that there were almost three billion gamers worldwide.[1] The average age of a male adult gamer is thirty-three and the average age for a female adult gamer is thirty-seven. There is an even distribution across age ranges, and an increase in 'older' players (defined as forty-one and over). In Australia, 67 per cent of the population play video games, and thirty-four is the average age of an adult player. Forty-six per cent of those players are female. Thirteen years is the average length of time adult players have spent gaming.[2]

Renowned game designer Jane McGonigal describes the fervour and energy of gamers:

> They are nine-to-fivers who come home and apply all of the smarts and talents that are underutilized at work to plan and coordinate complex raids and quests in massively multiplayer online games like *Final Fantasy XI* and *Lineage* worlds. They're music lovers

who have invested hundreds of dollars on plastic *Rock Band* and *Guitar Hero* instruments … They're young adults in China who have spent so much play money, or QQ coins … that the People's Bank of China intervened to prevent the devaluation of the yuan, China's real-world currency.[3]

There are also the parents challenging their friends to beat their top *Bejewelled* and *Candy Crush* scores; young women who style their dream homes in apps like *Home Design Makeover*; expats who stay in touch with family and friends back home by playing *Words with Friends*; seniors and retirees who have discovered that their old favourites, such as *Solitaire* and *Scrabble*, are digitised; and Twitter fans who got caught up in the viral game *Wordle*. If you don't fit into any of those categories, you might be one of the millions who have been sucked into games such as *Fruit Ninja*, *Bubble Poke* or *Angry Birds*.

And online gaming is big business. Smartphone gaming brings in about half of the total revenue for the gaming industry worldwide. Popular games, for example *Assassin's Creed* and *The Witcher*, have been turned into television series. Books get turned into games and vice versa, and the resulting products then get turned into movies, toys and adaptations.

But the real story around online gaming is how other technology companies have embraced features of games in their own platforms. Many addictive elements of games are now found in websites and apps, including progress bars, leaderboards, digital trophies and reward sounds. These game mechanisms encourage user participation and engagement. So thoroughly have companies embraced this that today you'd be hard-pressed to find a popular website or app without elements of gamification. Profiles scores on apps such as Uber and Airbnb, matches on Tinder, comparative statistics on Runkeeper, badges on TripAdvisor, trophies in Waze and profile achievements on LinkedIn are all forms of gamification.

We are gaming even when we don't realise it. Online algorithms use our preferences to shape our user experience, giving us intermittent micro rewards and boosts for our participation and providing progressive goals as we track our activities. I once worked with an academic who specialised in gambling. It was not too long after Facebook had introduced its news feed, with its infinite content and encouragement to endless scrolling. She remarked then on how much similarity she saw between the feed and pokies: the constant refreshing of new information delivers mini dopamine hits to our brains, similar to what happens in response to the bright chiming of the pokies.

Today's internet is basically one large game. If the mechanisms that make games so addictive are being implemented widely online without checks and balances, will we become a society of screen addicts? Or are we already?

Won't someone please think of ~~the children~~ everyone

While gaming has become an activity for all ages, a large proportion of gamers are still teenagers and young adults. Gaming allows an environment of play, exploration and inspiration, a space where young people can try new things and play out different roles. Some have built their entire social network through online gaming.

Patrick is twenty-three years old. Since his teens he has been a gaming addict. He and his high-school friends would play multiplayer shooter games such as *Call of Duty* and *Halo*. During marathon weekend sessions, they would clock up to fifteen hours a day.

Online gaming was the main way that Patrick and his friends spent time together. Their social network gradually expanded as the types of online games they played allowed for new players who could join from anywhere around the world. These new players would sometimes become friends, thus creating a tight social circle that was constantly replenishing. Patrick and his friends would also join global communities devoted to mastering these games, with enthusiasts creating wikis, websites and streaming channels to discuss the games. School, mealtimes and 'life' were irritations, momentary distractions from his gaming.

Patrick's mother was worried about the amount of time he spent gaming. She would regularly scold him about his gaming activity but never managed to persuade him to change his habits. It became a theatrical ritual between them: she would get annoyed and ask him to stop gaming or to take a break, then threaten to take away certain privileges, then give up and walk away. He would promise to cut back or take a break soon, then defy her openly, then claim victory as she conceded. It wasn't until she fell ill and was diagnosed with leukemia, when he was only eighteen, that he began to reflect on his gaming habits. She tragically lost her battle with cancer and passed away later that same year, and Patrick was forced to reassess his priorities. Four years later Patrick is still a gamer, but he looks back at that period with sadness and regret. 'I wish I had just listened to her and spent more time with her instead of online,' he told me. When I asked him why he spent so much time online in the first place, he replied, 'It's more fun than the real world.'

David, twenty-four, is ambivalent about his gaming habits. Online gaming has introduced him to a group of friends who look past his perceived language difficulties (English is his second language) and help him to be him more outspoken in his views. Yet he recognises that those views are often 'more toxic' than they once were. Spending upwards of 100 hours a week on multiplayer games such as the *Planetside* series (first-person-shooter games) and *Valheim* (a survival game based on Norse mythology) is still not enough for him: he benchmarks the time he's logged against professional gamers, who earn money from their habit. He shares Patrick's view that gaming is simply 'more fun' than real life and wants to challenge the negative public perception of online gaming.

It's hard to argue against this sentiment. Games are designed to be fun; everyday reality is not. Immersive games such as those Patrick and David play also allow the gamer to try on a different identity. In fact, the sheer pleasure and fantasy involved in adopting an online avatar is the secret to the success of these games. Game designers understand that playing a character in a virtual world has an irresistible allure for many.

The Sims is one of the best-selling video games of all time – it has sold approximately 200 million copies globally.[4] Developed by Maxis and published by Electronic Arts, it is a virtual dollhouse where players can create characters called 'Sims' and lead them through their lives, careers and relationships. It is a fun and addictive simulation of life. The game is largely a sandbox, meaning players can create, modify and destroy the environment to suit their (and their Sims') tastes. The term was derived from the idea of children's sandboxes, where they build and destroy the environment around them.

Players can customise their Sims in elaborate detail, choosing their features, hairstyle, outfits, voices and personality traits. They can build a small apartment or a huge mansion for their Sims. Career options for Sims are exciting, from secret agent to astronaut to celebrity to criminal mastermind – no bank tellers or public servants here. Some players relish the technical detail and the creativity of building homes and a community for their Sims, including cinemas, gyms, parks and restaurants. Others prefer to play out elaborate character narratives. And others, unsurprisingly, act out variations and snippets of their own lives, often as idealised or 'better' versions of reality.

I am a *Sims* player. My approach is to focus on narratives for a range of characters, and I let the personality traits 'guide' the resulting scenarios and interactions. This probably reflects my interest in psychology and sociology – I love to try to understand and predict how different characters will interact based on their inherent personality traits and backgrounds and the environments surrounding them. Still, there always seems to be one character that is oddly like me in appearance and mood, who ends up developing a relationship with a Sim who looks a little like my partner. There is also a variant of that character who is more reckless and freewheeling – perhaps a part of myself I wish I had the courage to reveal more often.

Sherry Turkle, a professor who specialises in psychoanalysis and human behaviour with technology, interviewed teenagers who lived out their lives in *The Sims* in different ways. Trish, 'a timid and anxious thirteen-year-old', has been 'harshly beaten by her alcoholic father': 'She creates an abusive family [but] in the game her character, also thirteen, is physically and emotionally strong. In simulation, she plays and replays the experience of fighting off her aggressor.' Rhonda, a 'sexually experienced girl of sixteen', creates an 'online innocent': 'She gets practice at being a different person … [her] character in *Sims Online* has boyfriends but doesn't have sex. They help her with her job.' Rhonda characterises her experience with *The Sims* as a chance to 'have a rest' from sexual expectations and reinvent herself.[5]

It's not hard to see why we enjoy playing games like *The Sims*. We're able to control, design and edit our Sims' lives as we see fit. It's easy to project versions of ourselves onto those Sims, as we give them personality traits and physical features we wish we possessed and propel them to take actions in their lives we wish we could carry out in our own.

It's this sheen of fantasy that can lead some gamers to develop addictive and destructive tendencies. In *The Cyber Effect*, Mary Aiken, who draws on psychology, criminology and technology to investigate how humans use technology, examines how gaming has caused pathological behaviours in some people. Dr Aiken highlights the fact that the American Psychiatric Association added compulsive online gaming to the official list of disorders in the *Diagnostic and Statistical Manual of Mental Disorders* (the DSM) in 2007. The DSM is the global standard for psychiatric diagnoses, and it informs and influences the entire healthcare industry. 'When the APA identifies a new clinical disorder, it's a big deal ... a game-changing event for mental health practitioners, patients and their families. It is a decision meant to stand the test of time, an acknowledgment that a behaviour has been consistently proved by studies to be serious and is understood well enough for criteria for diagnoses to be established and proper medical intervention and treatment options suggested,' writes Aiken.[6]

In June 2018, this categorisation gained global currency when the World Health Organization officially classified gaming addiction as a mental disorder – although not without some criticism and accusations of a 'moral panic'. The WHO added the condition to the eleventh edition of the *International Classification of Diseases* (ICD-11). The ICD-11 is used by medical professionals around the world to diagnose conditions and aims to encourage countries to develop public health strategies to combat these conditions. In it, the WHO defines gaming disorder as a 'clinically recognizable and clinically significant syndrome, when the pattern of gaming behaviour is of such a nature and intensity that it results in marked distress or significant impairment in personal, family, social, educational or occupational functioning'. It's worth noting that the WHO does specify that the disorder is rare and relates to the balance of activity in a gamer's life rather than only the amount of time spent gaming.[7]

South Korea has revealed cases of particularly destructive gaming disorders, resulting in tragic consequences. In South Korea, gaming is professionalised and some can make a living out of 'going pro'. The nation hosts ten pro-gaming leagues, most of which are broadcast on national television. At least two networks show 24/7 e-sports gaming coverage – players can win prize money of up to $250,000 as well as lucrative sponsorship deals. There are more than 20,000 internet gaming cafes, or 'PC bangs', around the country, designed to host marathon gaming sessions. These venues have come under scrutiny after an unemployed married couple became so hooked on a role-playing game called *Prius Online* – a virtual world where they were raising a virtual baby named Amina – that they neglected their actual baby, who had been born prematurely. *The Guardian* reported that the couple came home after one twelve-hour gaming session to find that their malnourished three-month-old daughter had died. 'I am sorry for what I did and hope that my daughter does not suffer any more in heaven,' the husband was quoted as saying. The newspaper also reported that a young Korean man was charged with murdering his mother to stop her nagging him for spending too much time playing games. Officials claimed that after her death he went to an internet cafe and continued with his game.[8]

While these extreme cases are statistical outliers, the conversation around problematic online gaming is gaining pace around the world. In April 2019, Prince Harry made headlines for something he's not usually associated with. Speaking at an event in West London, he called for the popular game *Fortnite* – which is aimed at children aged thirteen and older – to be banned. 'That game shouldn't be allowed. Where is the benefit of having it in your household? It's created to addict, an addiction to keep you in front of a computer for as long as possible. It's so irresponsible. It's like waiting for the damage to be done and kids turning up on your doorsteps and families being broken down,' he said. This accusation came as *Fortnite* enjoyed vast global success, with more than 200 million registered players worldwide. While *Fortnite* appeals to a younger demographic, it's not only children who are becoming addicted. Research conducted by Divorce Online in the United Kingdom showed that 200 divorces since January 2018 cited addiction to *Fortnite* as the cause of the relationship breakdown.[9]

Online multiplayer games such *Fortnite* cannot be paused or stopped until you've completed your mission or killed every other player in that session, so it can be a relentless, kill-or-be-killed scenario. Many combat-themed games that involve conquest and attacking other players for materials run around the clock. Players from different time zones around the world will be online while you might be asleep, so to protect your territory you need to put up in-game shields or else risk losing all the bounty you've collected. This is clearly an excessive demand on any player, yet it is standard across the genre.

As with gambling, the line between immersive gaming and addictive gaming can be a fine one. The world-building, the progressive rewards and the constant feedback loops all involve elements of behavioural psychology and classical conditioning techniques. Game developers need to acknowledge that there is the potential for their work to bring about real harm and should build in controls to minimise this risk. A report by the Australia Institute's Centre for Responsible Technology found that gambling-like features, as well as overt gambling, are common in games but are largely not recognised as such. The report found four types of crossovers between gambling and gaming.

- **Immersive and addictive technologies.** These employ the same features as pokie machines: intermittent rewards, no real sense of progress or levels, a lack of player agency and the ability to conduct microtransactions. These mechanisms foster addiction and can encourage players to spend too much time or money on the game.

- **Simulated gambling.** These are free games that mimic real-world gambling, such as virtual slot machines or card games like poker. Players gamble to win prizes. These are becoming particularly prevalent in mobile-phone apps, and they normalise and romanticise gambling and casinos. In some cases, these games even promote gambling venues and companies.

- **Purchase of chance-based items.** An increasing number of online multiplayer games are encouraging players to buy items such as 'loot boxes'. Loot boxes are mystery bundles containing in-game items (for example, rare weapons and armour, extra boosts and benefits, custom characters) that players can purchase using real money. A study on game platform Steam showed that the share of players playing games with loot boxes increased from 4 per cent to 71 per cent between 2010 and 2019. Loot boxes share important structural and psychological similarities with gambling, which could enable future problem gambling in children.

- **Actual gambling.** In some games, players can bet on the results of certain matches or games of chance using virtual currency that has a real-world monetary value. It can leave players open to unscrupulous operators and scammers.[10]

Brad Marshall is a Sydney-based clinician who specialises in treating children and young people who have internet and gaming addiction disorders. He is also a researcher furthering academic research on the latest treatment for these disorders. Marshall is a passionate advocate for raising awareness around these disorders, speaking regularly to teachers, students and parent networks, and at conferences. He laments the rates of gaming addiction in Australia and the low levels of public awareness about the disorder. Clinicians working in this field are a rarity, he tells me; only very recently has it been treated as a legitimate specialisation. He likens the slow progress in the recognition of gaming disorders to the recognition of other health concerns such as gambling and sugar addiction, which also took decades. The DSM classification, as well as research that uses functional MRI scans, have helped to quantify the effects of gaming and screen time, and this is encouraging people to take the issue slightly more seriously than in the past.

Marshall describes two pivotal studies that have contributed to the growing awareness of screen activity and addiction in online games. Both show that excessive online gaming can literally change the brains of young people.

Researchers from Finland found that knowing you're playing against another person (rather than a computer) activates a positive response in the brain. It did not matter if the other player was nearby or across an ocean – the mere existence of a fellow human provoked this response. This finding has implications for online games – multiplayer games, for instance, can trigger a heightened sense of social presence and activate the brain's reward system, prompting the release of dopamine. The research found that even brief game events triggered this reward system. Repeated exposure to this type of environment, therefore, results in repeated activation of our brain's reward system, potentially leading to addiction.[11]

A study using functional MRI scans found that screen activity (regardless of what that activity was – whether game-related or otherwise) influenced developments in the brain's frontal cortex, which controls higher cognitive function. It showed that high levels of screen activity resulted in thinner frontal cortexes in adolescents.[12]

Marshall is highly critical of Australia's capacity to treat gaming and screen disorders. 'There are hundreds of thousands, likely millions, of kids out there undiagnosed and not getting the treatment they need,' he says. Beyond private practices like his, there are hardly any public resources available, he tells me. This disadvantages families who are not able to afford private treatment. Educational resources are scant and research funding lacking, with the few academics who work in this space struggling to secure funds. Government initiatives tend to focus on cybersecurity or cyber abuse. The eSafety Commissioner, which provides resources on online abuse for victims and schools, is one such example.

Marshall points to specific features of online gaming that can be fraught with danger, especially for younger people, including in-game shopping features. He also highlights the ease of access to games on mobile phones, and the ease of playing them, with internet companies increasingly offering customers more bandwidth. He calls social media platforms 'dopamine labs' that exploit the micro rewards and dopamine hits associated with gamification to compel users to spend as much time as possible glued to the screen.

Marshall is a new breed of clinician who treats online disorders seriously and advocates for society to examine their impact. As we increasingly live our lives online, we need to recognise the problems that can stem from being always-on, including addiction.

I ask Patrick, our 23-year-old gaming addict, what he thinks about clinical treatment for his excessive gaming. Could it have made a difference to his behaviour, now or in the past? 'I don't know,' he says ruefully. 'All I know is that I wish it didn't take [my mum dying] for me to even think about it.'

There's more to the story

Although online gaming can lead to problems, it can also provide safe communities where gamers can explore, play and express themselves in fictional universes. Because players most often have an avatar, who they are in the physical world becomes secondary. Players can be free to act authentically, and their personalities – rather than their appearance – drive the interactions with others.

Online multiplayer games, including massively multiplayer online role-playing games (MMORPGs) such as *World of Warcraft* and *League of Legends*, are a hotbed of diversity and discovery. Gamer communities are often composed of players from around the world, spanning different age groups, classes and education levels. And through gaming, these otherwise disparate individuals form guilds, clans and tight-knit communities of interest. A 2018 survey by analytics company Qutee showed that more than 67 per cent of gamers have met up to five different friends while playing games, and another 37 per cent say they have met even more.[13] For millions of players, these games are places where they find their tribe, a group who accept their virtual selves as a dimension of their real selves. MMORPGs and social networking games encourage pro-social behaviours.

Developmental psychologist Isabela Granic led a study that describes how, 'in these virtual social communities, decisions need to be made on the fly about whom to trust, whom to reject, and how to most effectively lead a group'. There is evidence, she suggests, 'that social skills players learn within social online video game environments translate to real-world interactions'.[14] Co-op (or 'cooperative') games are specifically designed so that players need to form teams to progress. This is different from traditional multiplayer games, which pit players against one another. In popular co-op games such as *Borderlands*, *Diablo* and *Call of Duty*, players must actively work together to fulfil in-game objectives. A Pew Research Center study found that two-thirds of young gamers who enjoyed playing regularly did so to socialise with their friends and family. These type of pro-social behaviours are shown to affect children in their overall school activities. According to Granic, one study showed that 'children who played more pro-social games at the beginning of the school year were more likely to exhibit helpful behaviours later that year. When games have both pro-social and civic experiences (like building towns and communities), it would encourage civic activities in school as well, like volunteering, participating in school elections and fundraising.'[15]

The recreation elements of gaming are as important as the social. In 1975, Hungarian-American psychologist Mihaly Csikszentmihalyi pioneered the concept of 'flow', a 'state of concentration or complete absorption with the activity at hand': 'It is a state in which people are so involved in an activity that nothing else seems to matter.' It is the 'satisfying, exhilarating feeling of creative accomplishment and heightened functioning'.[16] This phenomenon of 'being in the zone' or 'finding a groove' can happen at work or while doing domestic chores. It can occur during physical activity, such as working out or swimming, or in the middle of a mental task, such as writing or solving a problem. 'Flow' is a desired state, and the concept has found its way into the language of many life coaches, teachers, managers and organisational designers. Flow can be difficult to achieve in everyday life but gaming and game-like activities can help to foster it.

There is a reason why millions are participating in games, and why, in some unfortunate cases, it turns addictive. It's because gaming absorbs you completely: creatively, mentally, emotionally and sometimes physically. Gaming demands that you are wholly present and focused on the task at hand, and it rewards this focus and attention regularly. As you progress through a game, your tasks become larger and more challenging, but you are given better tools to address those challenges, so you become more motivated to meet them. This process of 'levelling up' can be an intoxicating experience. In gaming, there are always defined, motivating tasks to perform that help a player's gameplay to evolve and improve. Each element of the game world is designed to encourage a player to progress. Edward Castranova, a leading virtual worlds researcher, says that 'there is zero unemployment' in *World of Warcraft*. 'The WoW workflow is famously designed so that there is always something to do, always different ways to improve your avatar.'[17]

In addition, in stark contrast to other aspects of our online lives – where we present idealised, empowered versions of ourselves – gaming allows us to make mistakes, in an environment with little judgement. Games are designed to have complex quests and challenging missions. Some in-game puzzles delve into rich lore and deeply developed histories and demand careful planning and strategy. Nicole Lazzaro, a researcher who looks at gameplay emotions, has been a design consultant in the games industry for twenty years. She reminds her readers: 'gamers spend nearly all of their time failing. Roughly four times out of five, gamers don't complete the mission, run out of time, don't solve the puzzle, lose the fight, fail to improve their score, crash and burn, or die ... When we're playing a well-designed game, failure doesn't disappoint us. It makes us happy in a very particular way: excited, interested and, most of all, optimistic.'[18]

Researchers at the Helsinki School of Economics and the Media Interface and Network Design Lab in the United States conducted research in human–computer interaction and cognitive science. They found that players get pleasure out of failing in games, particularly if the effect has a dramatic payoff, such as a cinematic animation sequence, because it builds the concept of the player's agency and control over the in-game universe. In the virtual world of the game, failure is accepted but not mourned. Gamers know that rewards are only several failures away. In games, we enjoy levelling up as much as we enjoy the struggles of getting there.

Not only do we enjoy levelling up, but we also enjoying doing so together and at scale. Gaming encourages the kind of wide-scale mass collaboration previously restricted to corporations, governments and religious groups. In his book *Here Comes Everybody*, Clay Shirky writes about society's 'latent groups', communities of people interested in niche topic who did not always have a chance to connect before the internet arrived. Getting thousands, let alone millions, of people working together on a task is hard, and very expensive. In a pre-internet age, unless you were a large enough institution with an appealing enough motivation, you were unlikely to attempt it. 'For centuries, people collaborated massively only on tasks that would make enough money to afford those costs [of getting people together]. You could work together globally at building and selling profitable cars (like the Ford Motor Company), or running a world religion (like the Catholic Church), or even running a big non-profit that could solicit mass donations (like UNICEF),' he writes. The internet did away with the transaction costs of bringing people together, and so a more diverse set of interest groups emerged. This is why the internet is often described as 'democratising'.[19]

'10 billion kills' was a huge collective milestone for players of the science-fiction cooperative game *Halo 3*. A coordinated in-game campaign to defeat the enemy army took more than 500 days and involved thousands of players worldwide. Many such quests take dozens of groups working together over days or weeks in a coordinated manner across the globe. It may seem trivial, but this is a meaningful example of social participation among a vast community of networked people, all working towards solving challenging tasks and collaborating on complex problems. They are focused on specific and actionable problems, motivated to pursue the common good and not scared of failure. Importantly, no one is getting paid to do it. They do it because participating in the game gives them a sense of engagement and achievement, and collaborating enhances that feeling. So perhaps there is something positive that could be tapped into in this vast online world.

Addressing the addiction

While online gaming has some positive dimensions, excessive gaming is a recognised disorder. Brad Marshall prefers the term 'excessive use' rather than 'addiction' when talking about gaming and screen disorders. This is because 'addiction' has specific clinical connotations and treatment plans that may not be appropriate for this type of disorder. But whatever the term, Marshall and other psychologists working in this area identify a common thread: a lack of balance. If excessive screen time or gaming is causing a fundamental imbalance in that person's life, and interfering with work, school, family and real-world socialising, it might be time to get help from a qualified psychologist.

Gaming detoxes or quitting 'cold turkey' are difficult to sustain, largely because it is difficult to remove yourself entirely from the source of temptation – staying offline for any length of time is near impossible in today's world. Such interventions can also create hostility between parents or guardians and young people, as it turns the conversation into a zero-sum game. Aiming for balance – accepting that gaming can still be a part of an individual's life, if it is within certain parameters that prevent it from taking over – is usually a healthier approach.

What can individuals do?

Control the access point

Brad Marshall's book, *The Tech Diet for Your Child & Teen*, calls this the 'control the wi-fi' rule. Online connectivity increases access and exposure to potentially addictive games. As such, putting boundaries around internet access is a key way to help young people with a gaming disorder. Controlling the wi-fi connection places the guardian in charge, so they can reframe the conversation around internet use and gaming to focus on balance. Part of this may involve putting conditions around internet usage. A negotiation is an opportunity for both parties to reach a compromise they can live with, to determine a level of internet use that both guardian and child feel is fair and reasonable.

There are software products that can assist with controlling internet use, such as Koala Safe and Family Zone, which allow guardians to schedule access and set timers. This can be helpful because young people are generally more savvy users of the internet than their parents, and they can often get around safeguards or gateways that parents construct. But no amount of opportunistic hacking can alleviate a lack of connectivity.

For adults with no supervisory guardian or helpful friend controlling access, create boundaries around the access point for online activity – which is likely to be your smartphone. Smartphones have become insidiously invasive in our lives. Controlling smartphone usage may start by identifying situations where you don't need to reach for your phone. Do you need to take your phone on a short walk to the shops? Does it need to be on while you're sleeping? Do you need to be checking it at mealtimes? Do you need to be texting or scrolling when already on another screen – for example, if watching a movie? Creating a set of rules or guidelines for yourself around smartphone use will help limit your time spent gaming.

Make gaming a reward and not a right

Controlling the access point can be a great first step in reminding ourselves of the purpose of connectivity. The tricky thing with online connectivity is that beneficial and harmful uses all blend into one seamless virtual experience. What may begin as a productive use of the internet – for example, for children it may be homework or study – can transform with a single click into an idle session of gaming.

If we must work to achieve our leisure time, we will appreciate it more. Parents can treat gaming as a reward – access to games must be earned by first using time productively. For example, if children complete chores and homework, they earn a certain amount of online game time. This reinforces the idea of balance and encourages healthy boundaries. This principle can easily translate to adults. What chore, task, exercise routine or work priority have you been putting off or procrastinating about, choosing instead to grab your device and while away the hours? Restricting 'leisure' use of screens and making gaming a treat after essential tasks are done encourages you to value your time – and when you get the reward of sitting on the couch with your phone to play a game, you'll enjoy it all the more.

Schedule online and offline time into your daily routine

Most of us benefit from a routine of some sort – a regular set of actions and tasks baked into our day that provides a sense of structure and order to our lives. For children, this is particularly important as they learn how to balance competing demands on their time and establish a healthy mix of work and play.

Scheduling online time for children means there is context and control placed around the moments they access games. Guardians and children may together want to draw up a plan for weekly screen time, solidifying the commitment. Importantly, though, any such plan should also schedule in offline activities, such as going for a walk or playing sport. This reinforces the idea of balance – if a child can map visually where internet use fits into their lives, it will help them to develop a sense of agency over their internet use. The plan could also be used to monitor internet use – for example, weekly screen time could increase or decrease depending on their usage the week before.

Most adults need to navigate ever-increasing demands on our time. The narrative around technology is often that it is a time-saver, but for many of us, technology and automation have just made us busy in a different kind of way. Scheduling formal offline times for exercise, meals, focused work or study and socialising lays the groundwork for a routine that may become habitual in the long term.

Restrict gambling

There is evidence which shows that normalising gambling-like behaviours can facilitate problem gambling later in life.[20] Parents and guardians should be aware of the features in games that allow gambling or in-game purchases. Monitoring and controlling access to real-world funds (for example, credit cards) may be required with younger children. Older children could be encouraged to be savvy about in-game purchases that cost real money – and if any purchases are made, the funds should ideally come from the child's own funds rather than the guardian's.

For adults, more structured regulatory interventions may be necessary, which will be covered in the section on what governments and society can do.

Be aware of the seductive fantasy

Games have popularised the idea of an avatar – an alter ego. Whether it's a mustachioed Italian plumber fighting dragons to save princesses in *Super Mario Bros*, a pixel farmer who tills and sows virtual farms in *Farmville* or a hustler driving through crime-ridden streets in *Grand Theft Auto*, life is more exciting when you can pretend to be someone else. Avatars are now everywhere on the internet. On social media platforms such as Snapchat, *bitmojis* are cute cartoon versions of ourselves. Apple's version, *memoji*, is similar: a personalised avatar you can design yourself and use in iMessage. The metaverse, a complete virtual universe that Meta has declared to be its future, will encourage us all to have avatars.

Avatars are representations of who we think we are online and how we think we are best portrayed. The ability to create online avatars – and new personalities along with them – is one of the most intoxicating qualities the virtual world offers us. We can do away with physical limitations and flaws and present idealised versions of ourselves. But it is important to remember that no matter how attractive a virtual world may seem, it is a narrow and idealised slice of real life. If you are prone to the intoxicating effects of online worlds or find yourself slipping down a rabbit hole, recognise the impulse and take yourself offline. Do something that connects you to people in the real world, such as phoning a friend, going to the shops or taking a walk. A dose of offline reality may feel like grim medicine, but it will help you to gain perspective.

What can governments and society do?

Employ fatigue and overuse systems

Gaming gives us an excellent clue about why being online can be so addictive. Online gaming taps into our desires for play, interactivity, discovery and socialising to make activities and tasks more fun. Individuals can develop boundaries around the way they use their screens and aim for a greater balance in life between being online and off. However, it is not just about individual control. Gaming companies design games to be addictive. Implementing controls and limitations on game design to make sure online games reduce the risk of addictive behaviour is a critical part of the solution.

Most smartphones have controls an individual can set to minimise their screen time. For example, Apple's iPhone offers downtime schedules, app limits, communication limits and content restrictions.

In the same way that we encourage individuals to self-regulate, we should encourage game designers to think about players. Many of the largest games in South Korea and China have 'fatigue systems' that restrict rewards, connectivity or progress after too many hours spent gaming. In the United States, there are 'resting bonuses' that encourage players to log off with incentives such as double rewards after a certain time spent offline. Australian-manufactured games should include mandated fatigue systems, which are consistent across all devices. These fatigue systems could activate once certain time limits are reached. A player's internet connection could slow down, loading times and resolutions become slower and more irritating, and game progress be paused or limited. Alternatively, research could identify critical thresholds around the number of consecutive logins or game sessions within a set period, and restrictions could come into effect once those thresholds are reached.

Combat games or massive online multiplayer role-playing games that are constantly live should build in rest periods that allow users to switch off without fear of attack from other players while they remain idle. This demand to be online constantly is clearly excessive, and rest breaks are simple circuit-breakers that could disrupt this system.

Design products for balance and not 'stickiness'

Games, online platforms and smartphones are designed for maximum engagement, seamlessness and interactivity. Safety by design considers user safety and risks at the beginning of the product design process, rather than only once the product has been developed. Introducing friction into a product design is one way to employ safety by design. Friction is the opposite of seamlessness, which creates a too-engaging or too-easy user experience. Friction introduces obstacles in online interactions by requiring a user to perform additional steps or forcing them to wait before carrying on with an action. For example, when making an online purchase, a pop-up box may ask whether you're *really* sure you want to complete this transaction. This may be particularly useful for children, who may not be fully aware of the implications of each purchase or may make purchases accidentally.

Positive friction of this type benefits the user. It encourages a player who may not be thinking clearly to pause and reminds them that there is an important decision to be made – and that decision has consequences. Friction points like checks and prompts introduce circuit-breakers during periods of extended connectivity or potentially problematic usage.

Regulate gambling and gambling-like features in games

Simulated and actual gambling within online games need to be subject to similar regulatory controls to offline gambling. There are several changes that could work in tandem here.

First, gambling companies should be restricted from developing, owning and operating online video games, particularly any games targeted towards children. This one should be a no-brainer.

Second, there should be more transparency around in-game purchases that cost real money. Rather than using in-game currency for transactions, masking the monetary value of purchases, users should have to pay real dollars for their items. Spending caps could be introduced to ensure addicts and children do not accumulate large debts rapidly. And items sold in loot boxes or similar should be available to players elsewhere in the game – perhaps able to be won through demonstrations of skill – limiting the scarcity and rarity of these items. Gaming companies will obviously not want to put such limits on their own products, so governments should play a role by drafting legislation to ensure these safety measures.

There should also be mandated educational campaigns, similar to those we have for offline gambling, in and around the online gaming industry, creating more transparency about the use of gambling-like features in games. Gambling features could also factor into a game's classification, much like themes of violence or sexual content, meaning potentially higher ratings and restricted access for minors on games that promote gambling.

Invest in early intervention, education and rehabilitation resources

Despite the World Health Organization and the American Psychiatric Association defining problematic gaming as a disorder, there is still not enough mainstream recognition of the condition and few resources to help sufferers. Government initiatives focus on cybersafety and cyber abuse, as opposed to the addictive aspects of online gaming. Gaming and screen disorders require a greater level of investment in research, clinical resources and prevention campaigns. Government bodies should produce resources for parents, schools and community groups about internet-related disorders that can affect children and young people. Our lackadaisical attitude to gaming companies also needs to change. There needs to be broader recognition that online games can be designed to be safer. We can have online platforms and products that promote healthier, balanced usage if only we demand it of those who make money off our addictions.

Could there be a world in which we optimise games, screens and our online experience to minimise harm and the potential for pathological disorders such as gaming addiction, while maximising diversity, community, play and global collaboration? There is much potential to learn from what makes games so addictive and apply the learnings to the real world.

Mihaly Csikszentmihalyi argued that the 'failure of schools, offices, factories, and other everyday environments to provide flow' was 'a serious moral issue, one of the most urgent problems facing humanity'. Why do we spend most of our time bored and anxious, when games point to an alternative? The solution seems obvious to Csikszentmihalyi: 'create more happiness by structuring real work like game work ... Our most pressing problems – depression, helplessness, social alienation ... could be effectively addressed by integrating more gameful work into our everyday lives.'[21]

Already many software companies are benefiting from using game mechanics. As our work and leisure activities increasingly come to incorporate the virtual, there will be natural opportunities to build an element of gamification into our lives. But what about offline? Designing spaces to incorporate play, discovery, interactivity and socialisation is a good idea. Town planning, city design, architecture and engineering are areas where game-like features, promoting fun in our physical places, could be considered. Some ideas that have been explored by designers include stairs that play music as people walk up and down them, billboards that tell a story when someone interacts with them and play equipment in the middle of sterile streets – aspects that make the drudgery of everyday life seem a little bit lighter.

Our world has no shortage of challenges. In the years to come, we will be tested as we encounter more problems that cannot be limited to by geography. We are faced with climate change, ecological degradation, global terrorism, cyber warfare and mass human displacement. Our current models of incentive and motivation have proven woefully ineffective at mobilising collective and, often, government action on these issues. We need to find ways to motivate individuals and nations to take a coordinated, global approach to collaboration. Just maybe, the sophisticated mechanics of online games offer lessons for us here. But first we must slay the dragons.

The Naive Futurist

For many, technology is synonymous with innovation, inventiveness and modernisation. It is synonymous with progress.

We live in the age of the technophile. Clever coders and 'experience designers' negotiate high salaries in the marketplace. Big Tech companies have overtaken fossil-fuel behemoths as the richest in the world, commanding the top prices in the share market. Tech entrepreneurs become sages as others perceive them to hold special knowledge.

'Luddite' is a term used to disparage those who are allegedly anti-technology. In truth, the Luddite movement was spawned by textile workers fighting for better labour conditions, and against the exploitation and automation that rendered jobs obsolete. The fact that, to most, 'technology' equals good and 'Luddite' equals bad reflects how technology has won the public relations war.

In the near term, breathless media articles, TED Talks and *Wired* think pieces declare that we are on the verge of technological advancements that will change the world as we know it. The metaverse, blockchain technology, cryptocurrency and Web3 will all – if the pundits are to be believed – reshape our world.

There is a particular type of tech-utopian who believes all the hype by default. This person does not question whether the technology has potentially negative implications – or whether it should exist at all. This person is likely paid to amplify the wide-eyed worship and mindless adoption of new products spawned by technology companies. Let's call this person a 'Futurist'.

Who are these Futurists? They are the so-called experts on the metaverse who emerged seemingly overnight (given the term was only popularised by Facebook in 2021). They are zealous 'cryptobros' who preach the gospel of cryptocurrency despite having little knowledge of contemporary finance or blockchain technology. These are NFT (non-fungible token) evangelists who invest their life savings in cartoons of gorillas without properly assessing volatility and liquidity. Entire armies of these people have arisen in a rush to ride the wave of promise technological developments supposedly bring. Much like those who led the dotcom boom and bust of the 1990s, these tech evangelists have blind faith in what they believe are the latest world-changing technological developments that will make them rich, quick, and usher in a new era of progress.

I know this type well. I was once a Futurist, although I'd like to believe I was one with a modicum of sense. 'Futurist' was never my official job title, but I've held various positions over the years that involved nonsense terms such as 'innovation strategy', 'trendcasting' and 'future tech development'. For years I worked at creative agencies that pedalled the digital future to consumers – which promised nothing but growth, profits and cool gadgets. As a digital evangelist, I had an air of 'cool kid' exclusivity – I had my finger on the pulse of the latest trends. I followed the latest developments in technology obsessively and, whenever something shiny was reported, would hurry back, like a courtier with gossip, to my clients, letting them know how they could get in on it. I would be invited to conferences to speak well of certain platforms or products. Once, this involved an all-expenses-paid junket to Las Vegas.

At the Australian Broadcasting Corporation, I held a coveted role leading the organisation's digital and innovation strategy. This involved managing partnerships with technology companies such as Facebook, Twitter, Google and Apple. Many wanted such a remit: being the gatekeeper was a valuable position. The role also involved 'trialling' new products and features put out by tech companies and strategically assessing the potential benefits and pitfalls for the organisation. Often, people just wanted to focus on the benefits and forget about the pitfalls.

But even during my own techno obsession, I had reservations about Big Tech. I recommended that we make formal commercial agreements with Google and Facebook (my plan was similar to the News Media and Digital Platforms Mandatory Bargaining Code, which came into effect in 2021), rather than handing over the organisation's content and audiences to them wholesale. Initially, some scoffed at the idea. 'Those companies will never go for it – they're too big' was a common response.

Far too often, we believe nothing but good can come from tech companies, despite evidence to the contrary. And those in agency roles like the ones I had can peddle these narratives internally, adopting the Big Tech rhetoric unthinkingly, without asking questions. Today, these roles come in many shapes and sizes. Tech companies pay above market rates to former public-service insiders to infiltrate government bureaucracy and provide information on valuable procurement contracts. Former regulators are courted to become policy directors and lobbyists to defend Big Tech rather than hold them to account.[1] Thousands of creative types, 'strategists' and marketers continue to sell the dream of a tech utopia and conveniently ignore the problems of sharpening social inequity, political polarisation, internet addiction, disinformation and predatory online behaviour. They overlook the tech companies' transgressions when incidents make headlines. Are these Futurists simply naive or is something more complex going on?

The metaverse and mixed reality

When Facebook, Inc. announced in October 2021 that it would change its name to Meta and shift its strategy to focus on the metaverse, it sent a ripple not just through the technology world but across the globe. Such a significant change was a signal to the world that the 'metaverse' was what we all needed to wrap our minds around.

There continue to be conflicting ideas over what the metaverse exactly *is* – mostly because it is yet to be built. It is an end goal that Facebook, and now many other companies, are working towards. The closest characterisation of the metaverse comes from Neal Stephenson's 1992 science-fiction novel *Snow Crash*, which was once a favourite of Mark Zuckerberg's – to the point that it was required reading for early Facebook employees.[2] It is an imagined virtual space that is shared and global, a rich and immersive environment that combines elements of virtual reality, gaming, online commerce, blockchain technology, artificial intelligence and multimedia in a seamless virtual space that we can all inhabit. It is a 3D virtual manifestation of the internet, where 'cyberspace' becomes an actual space people can visit in order to connect, work, transact, get entertained, collaborate and communicate.

So many people and companies are clamouring to have their say on the metaverse because it is undefined and unrealised but it seems like a plausible and dynamic possibility. Yet several existing and emerging technologies must coalesce for the metaverse to be built as imagined. One of the key elements is virtual reality.

Although virtual reality has been around for decades, it has only generated mainstream interest in the last few years. Virtual reality is a simulated 3D world that users can explore and interact in, drawing on their senses. It is different to augmented reality, which is an enhanced reality that projects computer-generated images over a user's view of the physical world, and mixed reality, which combines elements of the virtual and the real and encourages interaction with both. But while the definitions for each form of amplified reality might be hard to keep straight, all three have one thing in common: the technology has had little long-term observable impact on society.

Yet even the underdeveloped version of virtual reality that exists today has problems. Researchers at the University of Vienna studied the effects of social isolation in VR and found an interesting dynamic:

> Each volunteer enters a virtual environment, a sunny park, where they were invited to play a game with two other people. For half the volunteers, the ball got thrown to them about a third of the time ... For the other half though, the game turned into a middle-school freeze out: after a minute or two, the virtual players simply stopped throwing the ball to the volunteer and wouldn't respond if the volunteer asked why ... The volunteers who were excluded later reported significantly more anger and uncertainty than the ones who were included – and those who thought they'd been playing with a real human were even sadder. Conversely, of those volunteers who had been included for the full game, those who thought they were playing with real people reported significantly higher self-confidence.[3]

The study made it clear that social virtual reality can induce stronger emotional responses than simply interacting with a character in a game.

The emotional impact also lasts beyond the experience itself, with the feelings of rejection or inclusion carrying through into reality: 'After each volunteer had gone through the VR experience, an experimenter dropped a pencil in front of them; the researchers kept track of how long it took volunteers to react and then pick up the pencil. Those who had been excluded took significantly longer to do both.' Essentially, our experiences of social isolation and inclusion extend to our virtual selves and are as visceral as if they were happening offline.

Our biases also extend to the virtual world in subconscious ways. In his book *Future Presence: How Virtual Reality Is Changing Human Connection, Intimacy, and the Limits of Ordinary Life*, the *Wired* journalist Peter Rubin describes an interview with a female gamer who was sexually harassed in virtual reality and had no means of defending herself short of disconnecting. Because the game had been developed by men, they did not build in controls against attacks of a 'physical' or sexual nature – simply because it never occurred to them that such attacks could happen.[4] It is unlikely this oversight would have occurred to a group of women developers. This is merely another example of how we replicate our offline behaviours in the virtual world. Virtual spaces should therefore have the same safety protocols in place.

There is also concern about how virtual worlds give us the ability to filter out information or select what we choose to see. It's not hard to imagine augmented reality technology being powerful enough to allow us to subtract or obscure information from, as well as add extra information to, our physical worlds. Much like an ad blocker on a website, this technology could be used to filter out parts of reality that we find undesirable. Dr Steve Mann is a professor of computer engineering at the University of Toronto. He defines this concept as 'mediated reality': 'Mediated reality ... allows us to filter out things we do not wish to have thrust upon us against our will ... we already mediate our reality while we're on the Internet by blocking out ads and even people with whom we no longer want to interact. Beyond advertising and other people, what else will we choose to remove or block?'⁵ This raises the notion that we might be able to block out poverty, homelessness, illness, frailty, violence. These are harsh but necessary realities, though – will technology that makes us more comfortable also make us less empathetic?

These examples raise broad questions about the design and capabilities of the technology. Moreover, who is best placed to design the controls and the functionalities for our future virtual and mixed reality experiences? How do we ensure we don't build in harmful features born out of ignorance or discrimination?

There has already been one recent example of a virtual community a bit like the metaverse. It was powered by avatars and aimed to provide an immersive and expansive universe as an alternative to the real world. Second Life is a 3D online game developed by Linden Lab. It's not a 'game' in the sense of the online games we considered in the Screen Addict chapter. There are no narratives to follow, no bosses to beat or objectives to pursue. It's markedly different from the simulation of *The Sims* because you play as yourself, using an avatar, rather than creating characters. It's also multiplayer, meaning you are connected to other players live and online at the same time. It's not meant as merely a simulation of life but as a possible alternative. You can build houses and property, go to events and venues, and purchase in-game items using the virtual currency of Linden Dollars, which cost real, offline dollars.

Second Life launched in 2003 and four years later reached a million registered users, which was an impressive figure at the time. It received praise from both users and other companies. As its avatars had no limits on biology, gender or appearance, users could be whoever or whatever they wanted. It attracted all sorts of people, allowing for any fetish, experiment or genuine connection to flourish without judgement. Essayist Leslie Jamison writes:

> Intellectually, my respect deepened by the day, when I learned about a Middle Eastern woman who could move through the world of Second Life without a hijab, and when I talked with a legally blind woman whose avatar has a rooftop balcony and who could see the view from it (thanks to screen magnification) more clearly than the world beyond her screen. I heard about a veteran with PTSD who gave biweekly Italian cooking classes in an open-air gazebo, and I visited an online version of Yosemite created by a woman who had joined Second Life in the wake of several severe depressive episodes and hospitalizations.[6]

Commercial entities even developed virtual malls that sold products, generating real revenue. Politically opposed groups attacked and fought one another at specific locations. People had Second Life weddings; still others had Second Life affairs. In other words, Second Life facilitated in its virtual world the many varied interactions we conduct offline, and some interactions which can only happen within.

While it was popular, Second Life was subject to similar challenges to today's technology platforms: issues around operational performance, data breaches and security, pornography and fraud copyright. It regularly breached laws that did not yet factor in online spaces. There was some hysteria about the technology itself, but it soon died down. Second Life is an interesting case study because it was an audacious attempt at a virtual space that was as immersive and as real as possible. To many, it felt like the precursor of an immersive technological existence.

Will the metaverse simply fade into obscurity as Second Life has done? (Ironically, Jamison suggests that Second Life was usurped by Facebook, as the number of Second Life users peaked just as Facebook began to gain traction.) Or will the public buy into this idea and help to create it? Either way, the Naive Futurists of today are already declaring it the next big thing and seem unwilling to reflect on the full social, psychological and ethical implications of the technology.

WTF is Web3?

We are at the dawning of what many believe to the beginning of the third phase of the web, or Web3.

Web 1.0 was cumbersome and clunky. It was characterised by a static internet that housed limited information and the technology had limited capabilities. However, it ushered in an age of global connectivity, instant connection and freely available information. As connectivity infrastructure improved, giving rise to significantly improved data processing and capabilities, we developed the ability to create more interactive and engaging content. Web 2.0 allowed us to tell better stories through higher-fidelity images and videos, and to engage and collaborate across various social platforms and portals. Many people think about Web 2.0 in reference to social media and the way it enabled a global democratisation of information and communication.

The original Web 3.0 was supposed to be characterised by smarter tools and ubiquitous connectivity that allows for our physical world, and the objects in it, to have virtual capabilities and seamlessly interact with minimal human intervention. Web 3.0 systems were to be characterised by interoperability, decentralisation, uninterrupted connection, open technologies, distributed databases and cloud services. A simple way to understand it is through the lens of the 'internet of things'. The 'internet of things' refers to everyday objects that are connected to the internet and can engage with one other. For example, your smartwatch tracks your movements during the day so it knows if you're dehydrated or hungry and can ensure your favourite meal is ordered from your favourite online shop and delivered to your smart fridge by the time you get home from work. Your smart speaker can tell you the day's weather and help you decide if you want to go into the office or work from home, where your work devices are connected to remote servers that allow you to access all the company's documents. Your smartphone automatically switches between news and your song playlist depending on where you are in your commute, as it knows your preferences.

Beyond individual uses, Web 3.0 systems of industrial production, manufacture and distribution would rely less on human intervention and would be able to run in a self-sustaining way as various smart technologies interacted. For example, Web 3.0 hardware could have sensors that continually monitored it and could alert separate data centres or watch towers when there was a fault so that engineers could gain remote access and fix any issues. Smart power grids could use advanced analytics and systems to monitor and control power switching and load transmission, maintaining an ideal efficiency and meeting power demands across cities while connecting suppliers, power companies, homeowners and utility companies. Advanced Web 3.0 robotics could perform various medical procedures, build new construction projects, and conduct military operations and network probes remotely, allowing them to stay autonomous. In these ways, our 'online' and 'offline' activities, systems and identities could be further and further integrated until the distinction between the two essentially became meaningless.

However, Web 3.0 has now been updated to simply 'Web3' – and more emphasis is now placed on the use of blockchain technology to decentralise the web and its systems. Web3 is to be defined by open-source technology using blockchain so that ownership, permissions and governance are decentralised. Some of the main ideas about Web3 are around cryptocurrency, individual ownership and self-governance.

Cryptocurrency is the fuel that powers Web3 as the main source of currency instead of traditional money. The distribution and exchange of cryptocurrency is powered through a decentralised computer ledger, or blockchain.

Individual ownership, or tokenisation, is the idea that the activities conducted in the Web3 world can be owned and tokenised by individuals – for instance, your message or image can be represented through a non-fungible token that has a value and can be used to transact. This has given rise to many cartoon avatars as NFTs being sold for millions of dollars online.

Finally, self-governance is allegedly the dream of Web3. Blockchain technology relies on a distributed network, which means there is in theory no need for centralised authorities with decision-making powers, such as governments, banks and other financial institutions, to be involved in financial transactions.

There are some enormous questions around Web3 – more questions than answers at present. The utopian – or dystopian, depending on your perspective – vision of a decentralised and self-governing system is at odds with our current societal structure. Who should have the opportunity to design this new world? Who should decide how it functions? Even though the systems are theoretically decentralised, the physical infrastructure that powers the web is not decentralised. What ethical and moral implications are being ignored, like questions around data agency and privacy? Many considerations of Web 2.0 were overlooked or only realised years later, and we seem determined to repeat the pattern. The most zealous advocates of Web3 are those with the means and resources to control this technology – venture capitalists, tech CEOs and software engineers. Given these same figures dominated Web 2.0, will we simply further entrench the same patterns of inequality and the problems with rogue operators we're facing in today's digital landscape?

Of course, the Naive Futurists of today don't care for any of those questions. They only hear the hype, the thoughtless promise of benefits, and they see the potential advantages for companies in being the first mover on any new piece of technology. The ethical, moral, social and political questions are falling on determinedly deaf ears.

Technologists on either side of the fence

Lisa is a marketer by trade but has been in the social media game 'since the dawn of Facebook'. She leads three digital agencies that provide brands with various digital marketing and promotional services. One of those, a newly created agency, is dedicated to offering marketing services in Web3, which includes the metaverse.

As the hype around Web3 and NFTs grew, Lisa felt it was a growing wave that she had to chase and try to ride. 'After listening to 40 podcasts on NFTs … from people like [advertising entrepreneur] Gary Vee … I told myself this is going to be massive,' she says.

Lisa and her business partner decided to create an agency based around Web3 largely to gain the edge in the market. The two thought they could carve out a specialisation in this new space as commercial brands were only beginning to become aware of the technology.

Lisa's interpretation of Web3, though, is surprisingly akin to what Web 2.0 was supposed to be. 'For me, it's about community, it's about brands being able to engage with their customers, talking directly to them, having a conversation,' she says with the tone of an expert pitcher. Her knowledge of NFTs and blockchain technology is not that of a computer engineer but she has the same tingling optimism as the Futurists she has been listening to on podcasts. 'It's about transparency – the blockchain [ledger] cannot be hacked and is fully transparent,' she enthuses.

When I ask her what services her agency offers clients, she says it's 'mostly NFT PR'. 'I tell my clients, just buy land in the metaverse, just develop an NFT ... because it's a free PR kick,' she says.

For Lisa, giants such as Meta declaring their investment in the meta-verse proves the concept's legitimacy and is a sign to dive in behind them. She does acknowledge that 'there are a lot of scams and rug pulls [cryptocurrency swindles] out there ... but for me, once you truly look into the space and properly do your research, then you'll realise just how massive it's going to be.'

While Lisa sees great opportunity in these new trends, Michaela sees only a cheap trick.

Michaela is a technologist with vast experience of how the web has changed since its inception. She has worked in startups, enterprise companies and non-profits. She now runs her own production company and is a seasoned tech entrepreneur.

Michaela, a contemporary of many of the web's earliest originators, has been exploring and tinkering with the internet since the early 1990s.

She was even responsible for creating one of the very first websites in Australia.

For Michaela, one of the biggest changes in the evolution of the web came when it shifted from a purely research-driven, non-profit exercise to a realm that was commodified and advertising-based. 'I can't overstate what a jump that was ... it was just a different world,' she reflects.

At the end of the long jump pit is where we currently find ourselves, with Big Tech corporations that are essentially advertising companies mining and selling our data for profit and allowing a raft of societal, social and political issues to go under-regulated. It is this shift that concerns Michaela when it comes to Web3, with this extractive, purely profit-driven mindset motivating big business to embrace the new phase of the internet.

Michaela's production studio does a lot of work in the virtual and mixed reality space – practical and tested applications of what the metaverse will be based on. She sees a lot of great opportunities for virtual community building, connecting and exploration in the metaverse – if only it wasn't dominated by Big Tech. She is scathing of Web3 and has chosen not to participate in any of the crypto-based, NFT-focused Web3 initiatives that are currently in circulation, declaring that she has 'never seen a better scam, something worse than a Ponzi scheme, and the worst technology for right now'.

Michaela, as a tech entrepreneur, has looked beyond the superficial possibilities of the technology and is doing what all responsible technologists should be doing consistently – critically analysing the ethical, social and political implications of this new technology. Michaela feels Web3 is a 'dangerous approach', which 'at its premise is about wanting people to distrust institutions'. Beyond the get-rich-quick schemes and the gamification of virtual space, she sees 'a structure that is demonstrably flawed', encouraging separation and dissolution at a time when we all need instead to come together, to lessen the political polarisation and promote more trust in our institutions.

When I ask her about the alleged promise of Web3 – a supposedly decentralised, open and egalitarian paradise free from governance and authority that fulfils the utopian vision for the original World Wide Web – she recalls her meeting with American developer Vint Cerf, dubbed one of the 'fathers of the internet'. 'All he wanted to talk about was engineering,' she says. In her opinion, engineers were 'were never meant to be put in charge of building future societies'. She points to a glaring limitation in how we currently build technology: technologists are assumed to have considered the broader moral and ethical implications of their systems, but of course, in most cases they are neither qualified for nor very interested in this.

Ultimately, Michaela sees all the hype and 'fruitloopery' around the promised new tech of the metaverse and Web3 as 'the perfect smoke-screen' for the same people who are currently in power to extend their wealth. She fears it will be nothing but an amplification of the extractive and exploitative technology systems of today – a far cry from the open, collaborative, science-based research version of the internet that she and its founders were privileged to experience.

Visions of utopia or apocalypse?

What is curious about future trends is that some catch the public imagination and become exceptionally popular, such as the metaverse and Web3, while others, arguably much more future-proof, are given less emphasis. Consider two other major theories about our technological future: the singularity and transhumanism. The singularity is a hypothetical point in the future where artificial intelligence becomes so advanced and progresses at such momentum that it becomes uncontrollable, resulting in wholesale changes to human society. Often it is taken to mean the point at which technology gains agency and becomes self-actualising, the point at which artificial intelligence becomes equal to or surpasses human intelligence.

Ray Kurzweil is a well-known American inventor and futurist who writes about AI, among other technology-related topics. He is currently Director of Engineering at Google. In Kurzweil's view, the singularity 'will represent the culmination of the merger of our biological thinking and existence with our technology, resulting in a world that is human but transcends our biological roots. There will be no distinction, post-singularity, between human and machine nor between physical and virtual reality.'[7] Kurzweil went as far as to predict that the singularity will occur sometime in the year 2029, only a few years away.

Transhumanism may be born out of the same hubris, but instead seeks to use technology to help humanity surpass our biological limitations. Mark O'Connell is an Irish journalist and author who went deep into transhumanism to understand it. He describes it as 'a movement predicated on the conviction that we can and should use technology to control the future evolution of our species': 'It is their belief that we can and should eradicate aging as a cause of death; that we can and should use technology to augment our bodies and our minds; that we can and should merge with machine, remaking ourselves, finally, in the image of our own higher ideals.'[8] O'Connell encountered many remarkable characters while undertaking his research, including people who paid a lot of money to be cryogenically frozen until there's technology advanced enough to revive their consciousness and transfer them into new bodies. He also met bio-hackers who surgically implant bits of technology into themselves as physical augments, and spiritualists who found something new to worship in the technological.

Both the singularity and transhumanism have believers among the most influential and largest technology companies of our time. Peter Thiel, co-founder of PayPal and a technology investor, has backed companies working in radical life extension. Google has a life sciences division which explores, among other things, technological augmentation for biological problems. Elon Musk and Bill Gates have both expressed concern about the apocalyptic implications of the singularity – both take it very seriously as a real threat. These tech titans are larger-than-life figures, and we admire them and take inspiration from them. But they are also distant, inaccessible, multi-billionaire moguls who don't seem to harbour many concerns about the ethical implications of technology. Should we trust them to ensure our greatest fears about technology are not realised, especially as we barely understand what those fears are yet?

Silicon Valley evokes innovation and inspiration for many, but for others it is a shorthand for mistrust, cynicism and fear. When you read about what some people in Silicon Valley are up to, you can't be blamed for feeling cautious. O'Connell describes Dimitry Itskov, a Russian tech multimillionaire in his thirties and the founder of the 2045 Initiative, which aims to achieve cybernetic immortality for humans by the year 2045. One of Itskov's projects was the creation of 'avatars' – artificial humanoid bodies controlled through a brain–machine interface, technologies that would come with uploaded minds. He also describes Bryan Johnson, who backs tech entrepreneurs 'working towards quantum-leap discoveries that promise to rewrite the operating systems of life'. These approaches seem to validate the theory of the human body as essentially an obsolete form of technology.[9]

It seems credible that Silicon Valley executives consider the human body in need of hacking and fixing to make it more efficient. After all, isn't that what they've done to our lives? With a few swipes, isn't a car poised to come and pick you up at a moment's notice? Aren't our meal cravings being satisfied by services that are so efficient we can have food delivered to our door on a whim? Haven't our sexual partners been delightfully parcelled up as dishes on a sushi train, for us to pick or reject at will? Haven't our minds been flooded by every available form of entertainment, anytime, anywhere to suit our every mood? Haven't our memories been outsourced to a collective giant database so that we don't need to retain specific information about anything anymore? Bit by bit, our lives are already being hacked and replaced by updated technology.

Consider the term 'cyborg'. For most people, it conjures up science fiction – a Robocop-type figure, half-human, half-machine, encompassing both but somehow lesser than either, inherently freakish. For others, it could be used as an insult, or generally has negative connotations – when someone displays a cold, robotic demeanour, they seem to lack empathy or warmth. Mark O'Connell challenges us to think hard about the term and what it means to each of us and to society:

> In a certain sense, the idea of the cyborg is no more less of a particular way of thinking about the human, a peculiarly modern picture of a person as a mechanism for the processing of information. Do you wear glasses? Do you wear orthotics in your shoes? Do you have a pacemaker fitted to your heart? Do you get a strange phantom limb sensation when you are for some reason denied access to your smartphone, when your battery's

dead or your screen is smashed or you left the thing in your other jacket, and so you can't access some other piece of crucial information, or you can't navigate via GPS, can't triangulate your location using a satellite orbiting the Earth? Are you therefore lost? Does that lostness, that loss, suggest a breakdown in the exogenously extended organization complex of your body and its supplementary technologies, a rupture in the homeostatic system of yourself? If a cyborg is a human body augmented and extended by technology, is this not what we basically are anyway? Are we not, as they say in the philosophy racket, always already cyborgs?[10]

What will it mean to be a person in these new technological worlds? Will we thrive in the metaverse, or be emotionally and socially stunted? Will we have more equality in Web3 or become further entrenched within unfair power structures? Will the singularity bring about a golden age of productivity and progress, or will we become slaves to machines? And will transhumanism be a boon or a curse for humanity?

Do Naive Futurists even bother asking these big questions, or are they just hype-mongers for big technology companies? Consider an example: Google Maps. Google took a *terra nullius* type of approach to mapping our homes, our streets, our neighbourhoods, our suburbs, towns and countries. Without permission, Google just went around in their little surveillance vehicles and captured our topographies for their own purposes. No one thought to question it because at the time we had limited awareness of its implications. Now, years later, we are much savvier about our data agency, data privacy and data ownership. Did Google have any right to do what they did? Should they have sought permission, given they did not own any of the data footprints they captured? For many of us, Google Maps captures our movements as well: our habits, our routines, where we like to eat, to shop. All the implications around incursions of privacy and data agency were not considered when Google Maps was first developed because the futurists and technologists were allowed to run these programs – with limited interventions from government and civil society groups.

In the new, bewildering worlds of the metaverse, Web3, the singularity and transhumanism, what rights will everyday people have against these vast technological forces? There is a philosophy shared among the tech elite that focuses on the potential value of future technology and vast societal changes brought about by technology. It is called longtermism. Longtermism is the view that we should support world-changing projects – such as the colonisation of Mars, space travel and the alleged changes Web3 will bring about – because the future value these will bring humanity justifies any potential disruption in the present or immediate future. Philosopher and author Émile P. Torres describes longtermism as:

> ... akin to a *secular religion* built around the worship of 'future value', complete with its own 'secularised doctrine of salvation' ... The popularity of this religion among wealthy people in the West – especially the socioeconomic elite – makes sense because it tells them exactly what they want to hear: not only are you *ethically excused* from worrying too much about sub-existential threats like non-runaway climate change and global poverty, but you are actually a *morally better person* for focusing instead on more important things – risk that could permanently destroy 'our potential' as a species of Earth-originating intelligent life.[11]

230

Longtermism has advocates in the tech barons of today – including Peter Thiel, Jeff Bezos and the incorrigible Elon Musk. For these men, the concerns of the present are only worth addressing insofar as they impact on their grandiose visions of the future. As Torres elaborates: 'Why does Musk care about climate change? Not because of injustice, inequality or human suffering – but because it might snuff us out before we can colonize Mars and spread throughout the universe.'

Longtermism broadly permeates the thoughtless tech worship of the Naive Futurist, who jumps at any declarations made by the tech egomaniacs of today with vague notions that they are doing things which will allegedly create future value for all of humanity, never once thinking of the cost born by the people and society of today.

The funny thing about the future is that it eventually becomes the present. Perhaps we should have 'present-ists' who factor today's problems into any new technological build. Perhaps, that way, these new technology phases will benefit us all, rather than being used for more exploitation, hot air and substance-less hype.

How to make the new phases of the web better

What seasoned technologists such as Michaela remind us is that the web has gone through multiple phases. The current version of the internet is only one iteration of it. Unfortunately, that iteration has been defined by a small handful of companies with an extractive business model that has caused many harms. With the new phases of the web being heralded by advocates and critics alike, it is incumbent on us to learn from previous mistakes and make sure we address current issues so as not carry them over into the future.

Already Big Tech companies are staking claims in Web3. Meta has the metaverse, Google is betting on AI and quantum computing, and former Twitter CEO Jack Dorsey is investing boldly in cryptocurrency. If the public, civil society and human rights groups do not intervene, these tech barons will continue to define the new phases of the web, and inevitably only a narrow few will benefit.

Addressing our present problems

The digital systems of today have some significant and unresolved problems. Big Tech companies continue to commit privacy incursions into our personal data and personal agency by tracking our behaviours, movements and locations. There is unwelcome surveillance in many of their apps and products. These largest tech companies have monopolistic structures that are harmful to economies and consumers. Social networks continue to violate human rights in vulnerable countries, with their platforms being used to support dictators and tyrants. Disinformation continues to run rampant on many online platforms, threatening democratic institutions, public health and the rule of law.

The litany of problems related to technology platforms are pressing. The most damaging companies, such as Meta, would like nothing more than for us to move on to the 'next phase of technology' – to pivot right into the metaverse. They hope that these new virtual worlds and systems will be untarnished by the problems that dog their older products. But we must not let Big Tech dazzle us into forgetting the persistent safety issues they have yet to address, because the same issues will just manifest in new and different, and perhaps worse, ways in those new spaces. Rather than simply embracing Web3 like Naive Futurists, we must hold technology companies to account.

What can governments and society do?

Regulation and governance

We are still grappling with the most effective way to govern the internet and will continue to do so over the next few years. As new technologies develop, the ongoing challenge and opportunity for humanity is: how can we best build an internet that is safe, fair and healthy for everyone?

The European Union is leading the way. The European Commission, the EU's executive arm, has found Google guilty of antitrust breaches in three cases since 2010 and fined the company over €8 billion. In 2017, it noted in relation to Google Shopping: 'Google has systematically given prominent placement to its own comparison shopping service … rival comparison shopping services are subject to Google's generic search algorithms, including demotions (which lower a search entry's rank in Google's search results).'[12]

The European Union has also implemented pioneering legislation such as the General Data Protection Regulation (GDPR) – the first wholesale regulation on data processing and data privacy in the world. Brought into law in April 2016, the GDPR is an important part of EU privacy law and human rights law, including the Charter of Fundamental Rights of the European Union. The *Digital Markets Act*, recently adopted by the European Council, seeks to ensure healthy competition in digital markets and prevent large companies such as Google from forming monopolies. It is a landmark bill that does away with lengthy antitrust investigations – though some Big Tech companies are finding loopholes to exploit.

Thirty-six states in the United States, including New York, Colorado and Arizona, have all experimented with some form of legislation and regulation of Big Tech, including through several antitrust cases against Google, Amazon and Meta. There continues to be some hope for action from the Federal Trade Commission, given chairman Lina Khan's stance on Big Tech monopolies. Khan is a vocal critic of Big Tech who first made waves with her antitrust paper on Amazon. This paper was widely credited with igniting debate on whether the country's current antitrust laws were sufficient to keep Big Tech in check.

Australia too has attempted to rein in Big Tech through legislation, but has not gone as far as other parts of the world. The divisive News Media and Digital Platforms Mandatory Bargaining Code came into effect in March 2021 and forces Google and Facebook to pay for local news content – but critics say it is geared to supporting large news organisations and does not do enough to support public interest journalism. The landmark Australian Competition and Consumer Commission Digital Platform Services Inquiry is due to deliver a final report in March 2025 – but progress has slowed after initial momentum. There have been many missed opportunities for progressive regulation at the federal government level. With a new federal government as of May 2022, there is an opportunity to focus on this important inquiry.

Regulation will inevitably lag behind technological developments but what's exciting is that we are entering a phase where technology companies can no longer assume they are exempt from the rules of the physical world. As more evidence of their lack of adequate safety protocols and their negligence comes to light, they can no longer deny the significant harmful impacts their platforms and products have on society. We must stay vigilant and continue to hold Big Tech to account with legislation, codes and mandates so that we can make progress on the issues of today, instead of leaving them to carry over into the new virtual worlds of tomorrow.

Safe, ethical and open technology design

Technologists have for too long been given a free hand to develop their products in isolation, without government oversight or any requirement to consider the broader implications of what they're building. In a world mediated by digital technology, this cannot continue. We have seen in previous chapters how wide-ranging and potentially harmful digital technology can be.

It is imperative that technological products are built with certain minimum standards of safety and ethical considerations in mind. Pharmaceuticals are rigorously tested for their effects before going to market. The automotive industry was required to have mandatory seatbelts and safety testing. Any new construction must comply with the relevant building codes and meet clear standards of safety and quality. In all areas of life except the digital world, we have standards of care and compliance. Digital technology products and platforms must not be exempt – they must also be subject to minimum standards. These need to include considerations for the principles of human rights and safe use. They also need to include a commitment to minimise bias and discrimination against specific minorities and groups, both in the design of the technology and among the communities on the platforms; procedures for banning and reporting user behaviour that compromises others' safety or is illegal; and transparency in product and algorithm design.

Governing bodies that sit outside the technology industry should have a degree of oversight over digital products, so that civil society, academia and human rights groups are consulted in the design of new products and consideration is given to factors beyond the commercial. Principles such as safety by design and privacy by design are recommended so that safe use and privacy features are built into software products from the beginning, and not just applied after products have been built and violations have occurred.

Ethics and ethical design should be compulsory modules in software development and computer science courses. This would give the engineers of the future a framework in which to consider the implications of the technology they are building. It would also encourage them to learn from the lessons of the past.

Ultimately, digital technology is too pervasive, and too integral in our lives, for us to allow a handful of rich Silicon Valley–based technophiles to have the only say in how the digital technologies of our present should be used and the digital technologies of the future should be built.

Kill the hero worship

Technology companies and the tech entrepreneurs that run them may hit the headlines regularly with amazing innovations and beta products that excite and delight us. But the creators of technology may not be the best people to develop the ethical, moral and political frameworks to interrogate their own products and services. That's why we have philosophers, authors, human rights advocates and technology activists.

One of the complications we currently have is that we allow tech moguls to weigh in on areas in which they often have limited expertise: federal politics, the environment, poverty, war and climate change. We must not conflate technological prowess with moral authority, engineering nous with leadership and coding skills with ethics. The most successful tech CEOs are almost invariably privileged white men who have led sheltered lives and often come from a very specific Anglocentric point of view. They are neither qualified nor cosmopolitan enough to dictate the global systems of tomorrow.

Michaela points out, very reasonably, that technologists are often concerned almost exclusively with a certain narrow set of problems focused on the construction and engineering of their technology. We should draw other, more informed voices into the debate as part of rolling out any new technology. This could include academics, journalists, the target users and civic rights groups. It is critical that more diverse perspectives are heard if we are to create a truly equitable and ethical online world.

Slow down and change the technology narrative

There is a popular line, attributed to American sociobiologist and two-time Pulitzer Prize winner E. O. Wilson, that is quoted frequently by technology thinkers and critics: 'The real problem with humanity is the following: we have Paleolithic emotions, medieval institutions and god-like technology.' It captures the chasm between our primitive brains, which have not evolved substantially since our *Homo sapiens* ancestors; our systems and institutions, which were mostly built centuries ago; and the staggering pace of our technological development, the speed and scale of which astounds us at times.

Our very human minds and emotions are not built to navigate such a rapidly changing world. What we need is time – to reflect on, reassess and review the vast technological architecture in our lives today. We need to study the various societal impacts of some of these technologies, create frameworks that ensure safe and healthy use of the internet, and develop standards to make sure our most vulnerable aren't bearing the brunt of the ill effects.

As we grapple with significant global issues – climate disasters, geopolitical instability and a swelling global population – we must reframe the narrative of humanity's technological development. In the longer view, it should not be a story of speed and scale and perhaps eventually destruction but one of balance, sustainability and communal wellbeing. As a wise soul once said, 'Slowly is the fastest way to get to where you want to be.'[13]

If technology is used to violate human rights, is that progress? If the web destabilises our democratic institutions, is that innovation? How can we say we benefit when technology monopolies become more powerful than elected governments? The starry-eyed technologists have had their naive visions of tech utopias brought crashing down as the Big Tech companies become embroiled in an ever-revolving series of scandals and social harms. If we are to use technology so that it benefits the majority, rather than enriching a small number of tech entrepreneurs, we must learn from our past mistakes. We need to put society at the centre of our relationship with technology and legislate accordingly.

Conclusion

It's April 2022. I'm in a conference room in Sydney's CBD at a seminar that promises to demystify Web3. The city is still relatively empty because of the Covid-19 pandemic but there are tentative signs of life returning, including this venue. An enclosed, windowless room full of strangers would have been unthinkable only a few months ago.

There are about seventy attendees, maybe a few more. I can't help thinking that, statistically, there must be at least one of the online types I have identified in this book among the guests. That sharp-suited professional-looking man could possibly be a Hateful Troll. The young woman who just took a selfie of herself – probably a Social Media Narcissist who will slather it across her social profiles. I turn sideways and the skittish-looking guy in his forties certainly suggests with his jittery fingers and darting eyes that he could be a believer in conspiracy theories – or perhaps he's just jonesing for a cigarette. I wonder if one woman who is clearly not bothered about social distancing and exclaimed loudly when she entered, 'Do we really need to wear *masks* for the whole thing?' is a Freedom Fighter. I amuse myself by thinking those focused on their phones are swiping on a dating app or messaging a potential hookup. Some will be playing games, of course.

I hope none of them is gambling – though chances are that someone is.

I am not judging any of them for their potential problems with technology – after all, I share some of these problems myself – but I have realised in writing this book these behaviours are far more common than we think. I set out to test the theory that we all know someone who has a problematic relationship with the internet, if we're lucky enough not to have one ourselves. The weight of evidence is clear. I didn't have to look hard to find the stories in this book, and there were many more people I interviewed whose stories I didn't include.

I heard from Anne, the Insta-mum I once considered a friend, recently. When I got married, she sent me a message via Instagram from an old profile of hers, which I had forgotten about. Perhaps she felt left out because I hadn't invited her to the wedding after such a long period of not speaking. Perhaps she had expected to be? It was surprising, but the message was pleasant, polite, so I responded. We made banal small talk for a bit, until inevitably the conversation turned to her latest sponsorship deal – she's *so busy* making content for a caravan manufacturer, she told me. After that, I let the conversation fizzle out, knowing how it would continue.

I also heard from Kylie, the Freedom Fighter who had her life turned upside down by the pandemic. She wanted to check in but also was trying to indoctrinate me into voting for the Palmer United Party in the upcoming federal election. The party claimed to champion the 'freedom' she and her tribe craved.

I wanted to hear evidence of change. But what I got was probably more realistic. The problems around technology use continue unabated, and in many cases unresolved. They have resulted in damaged relationships, hardened thoughts and radicalised viewpoints, and a deepening of the divides between people.

Conclusion

Is it fair that the largest technology companies continue to rake in massive profits year on year, without significant penalties, when their platforms are a source of long-term harm for some? Why do we continue to minimise and overlook online addiction and radicalisation, acting as though they have less urgency than other mental health problems?

This book is at once a warning bell and a call to arms. There is still so much to be done to stem an emerging mental health epidemic. People living in the grip of conspiracy theories they discovered online continue to have little specialist support and few treatment options. Their loved ones are left trying to guide them out from the murky dark of QAnon. Those whose lives were shattered by the pandemic struggle on as promised government support services continue to underdeliver. Online platforms keep promoting content and features that impact on our mental health, and our children's mental health, as unrealistic standards of beauty and body image are plastered across our social feeds. Angry young men who feel disconnected from their communities find unlikely allies online, who sometimes radicalise them to dangerous and criminal ends. Relationships continue to be altered by digital mediation as apps that promise to bring us together warp our experiences. And we continue to stare down into our screens, playing games for hours on end, without pause, without break, caught in addictive loops that compromise our health and our wellbeing. As we face even greater, more confounding and more powerful technological changes – like the metaverse, Web3, quantum computing and super-advanced AI – it might be time to do away with outdated notions of online versus offline. We are digital beings, just as much as physical beings.

We can all help in tackling these issues, whether by individual acts of self-monitoring and self-care, determined support for friends and family, brave moments of calling out behaviours online or standing up for the vulnerable. Seemingly small, inconsequential behaviours that won't be noticed or celebrated – being mindful of our phone use, unfollowing certain profiles, trying to connect and engaging in real life, checking information sources, relishing in a moment without posting about it, and limiting time on certain apps and platforms – will in time make a real difference to our lives.

We also need large, system-wide changes, at the institutional, governmental and global levels. Brave legislation, regulation that dares to challenge new technology, product design that cares about more than just profit. There are signs of such things. The European Union continues to push ambitious regulatory agendas to create a healthier, more competitive digital landscape, with progressive reforms such as the *Digital Markets Act* to combat tech monopolies and the recently passed *Digital Services Act*, which will make digital platforms take responsibility for their content. Australia's landmark Digital Platforms Inquiry, developed by the Australian Competition and Consumer Commission, continues to push recommendations that will make meaningful differences, if only the federal government has the vision to act on this advice by developing appropriate legislation.

In April 2022, the White House released a Declaration for the Future of the Internet, a manifesto that promises an internet that is open and competitive, protective of privacy and respectful of human rights. The declaration highlighted several principles, including commitments to:

- protect the human rights and fundamental freedoms of all people
- promote a global internet that advances the free flow of information

- advance inclusive and affordable connectivity so that all people can benefit from the digital economy
- promote trust in the global digital ecosystem, including through the protection of privacy
- protect and strengthen the multi-stakeholder approach to governance that keeps the internet running for the benefit of all.[1]

The declaration has been signed by sixty fellow nations from around the world. Whether these good intentions translate into action remains to be seen, but it's an achievement to get multiple countries around the world to agree on a new approach to technology.

On the ground, there are resilient rights groups, civil society organisations, researchers and campaigners who continue to push a rights-based agenda in relation to technology, calling out Big Tech's transgressions, lobbying for change and creating compelling narratives to push for action.

Finally, the public are learning more about the harms of Big Tech, with survey after survey revealing that people want stronger action from technology companies, more ambitious regulation from government and better support and education for those struggling with mental health, exacerbated by time spent online. On social media platforms, more are sharing stories about how we can be better online citizens, and everyday acts of resistance – calling out bad online behaviour, disconnecting from toxic platforms, encouraging frank discussions about body image – are helping individuals to question, reassess and shift their attitudes.

I get in touch with Ash Jackson, the reformed Freedom Fighter we met in Chapter 2, some months after our conversation to see how she is going. Ash has taken back her life. She's working at a club, which she enjoys, not as a musician but still part of the entertainment industry. Her Freedom Fighter comrades are all but forgotten. When I ask her if she thinks about them, or the movement more broadly, she shrugs and says, 'Not really.' Some of the ringleaders are facing criminal charges for their protest activities. She feels that certain individuals in the freedom movement are dormant but not defeated. 'I think they're waiting to see what the next moment is that they can latch on to,' she says. Still, Ash's story is one of hope, tenacity and perseverance, showing the kind of difficult, sustained effort that is needed to claw your life back from the digital abyss. Despite being drawn deeply in by the lies and manipulations of the freedom movement, Ash won out in the end and took control of her situation.

Times of upheaval always present the opportunity for change. Let us not allow the powerful tech barons to define what our digital future looks like. It is time we took back our agency and created a new approach to our digital future – starting now.

Acknowledgements

I am indebted to those who chose to share their stories with me, no matter how painful or challenging they were. I hope that through this book, you'll come to realise just how many others share your struggle.

All those who shared their stories spoke to me freely and without payment. The names and, in some instances, locations and identifying details of individuals have been changed to protect their identities. These are common stories, and any similarities to individuals I did not speak to for this book are purely coincidental and unintentional.

Thank you to the academics, researchers and subject specialists who shared their insights and expertise with me. Your work is invaluable.

I am grateful that my manuscript came across my publisher Julia Carlomagno's desk at Monash University Publishing. She understood the vision for the book and its potential, and helped me to realise it. Thank you also to the rest of the team at Monash University Publishing.

Thank you to Peter Lewis, the driving force behind Centre for Responsible Technology, who was not only open to discussing issues around technology but was also willing to do something about it.

The Australia Institute deserves special recognition for allowing me to be part of their fiercely talented team – researchers, intellectuals and public-policy powerhouses who influence our national conversation. I am in awe of you for constantly putting the 'tank' in 'think tank'. Royalties from this book will be donated to the Australia Institute to continue their valuable work in this area.

Finally, this book would not have happened without unwavering support from my family and friends – my partner, Tim, who shares my journey; my family, for never tiring of my eccentricities; and my friends, especially Marisa and Ryville, who helped ground and refine my ideas with their graceful company and debate.

The conversation about our use of technology and the role of Big Tech is a critical one. I hope we not only continue it but also take decisive action to bring about a safer and healthier digital future for all.

Resources

Mental health and support services

1800Respect, 1800respect.org.au

Beyond Blue, beyondblue.org.au

Black Dog Institute, blackdoginstitute.org.au

Butterfly, butterfly.org.au

Gambling Help, gamblinghelponline.org.au

Head to Health, headtohealth.gov.au and headtohealthvic.org.au

headspace, https://headspace.org.au

Lifeline, lifeline.org.au

MensLine Australia, mensline.org.au

MindSpot, mindspot.org.au

Phoenix Australia, phoenixaustralia.org

Reach Out, au.reachout.com

Sane Australia, sane.org

This Way Up, thiswayup.org.au

National mental health hotlines

Australian Capital Territory: Canberra Health Services Access Mental Health, 1800 629 354 or 02 6205 1065 (available 24/7)

New South Wales: Mental Health Line, 1800 011 511 (available 24/7)

Northern Territory: Northern Territory Mental Health Line, 1800 682 288 (available 24/7)

Queensland: Mental health access line, 1300 642 255 (1300 MH CALL, available 24/7)

South Australia: SA Covid-19 Mental Health Support Line, 1800 632 753 (available 8.00am to 8.00pm)

Tasmania: Mental Health Services Helpline, 1800 332 388 (available 24/7)

Victoria: Head to Health, 1800 595 212 (available 8.30am to 5.00pm, Monday to Friday)

Western Australia: Mental Health Emergency Response Line, 1300 555 733 (metro) or 1800 676 822 (Peel) (available 24/7)

Online safety

eSafety Commissioner, esafety.gov.au

For children and parents

Kids Helpline, kidshelpline.com.au

Parentline New South Wales, parentline.org.au

Parentline Northern Territory and Queensland, parentline.com.au

Parentline Tasmania, health.tas.gov.au/service-finder

Parentline Victoria, services.dffh.vic.gov.au/parentline

Parents South Australia, cafhs.sa.gov.au/services/parent-helpline

Parents Western Australia, wa.gov.au/service/health-care/public-health-services/ngala-parenting-line

Raising Children, raisingchildren.net.au

Notes

Introduction

1. Alexis Madrigal, 'Who's really buying property in San Francisco', *The Atlantic*, 20 April 2019.

2. Shirin Ghaffary, 'Even tech workers can't afford to buy homes in San Francisco', *Vox*, 19 March 2019.

3. Adam Brinklow, 'UN report calls Bay Area homeless crisis human rights violation', *Curbed*, 26 October 2018.

4. Georgia Wells, Jeff Horwitz and Deepa Seetharaman, 'Facebook knows Instagram is toxic for teen girls, company documents show', *The Wall Street Journal*, 14 September 2021.

5. Examples of external research include: Mary Sherlock and Danielle Wagstaff, 'Exploring the relationship between frequency of Instagram use, exposure to idealized images, and psychological well-being in women', *Psychology of Popular Media Culture*, vol. 8, no. 4, 2019, pp. 482–90; Claire Midgley et al., 'When every day is a high school reunion: social media comparisons and self-esteem', *Journal of Personality and Social Psychology*, 27 June 2020; and Alexandra Lonergan et al., 'Protect me from my selfie: examining the association between photo-based social media behaviors and self-reported eating disorders in adolescence', *International Journal of Eating Disorders*, 7 April 2020.

6. Craig Timberg, Elizabeth Dwoskin and Reed Albergotti, 'Inside Facebook, Jan. 6 violence fueled anger, regret over missed warning signs', *The Washington Post*, 22 October 2021.

7   Cat Zakrzewski et al., 'How Facebook neglected the rest of the world, fueling hate speech and violence in India', *Washington Post*, 24 October 2021; Alexandra Stevenson, 'Facebook admits it was used to incite violence in Myanmar', *The New York Times,* 6 November 2018; No author, 'Facebook approves adverts containing hate speech inciting violence and genocide against the Rohingya', *Global Witness*, 20 March 2022; Sebastian Strangio, 'Facebook fails to detect hate speech against Rohingya, report claims', *The Diplomat*, 22 March 2022; and Roli Srivastava, 'Facebook a "megaphone for hate" against Indian minorities', *Reuters*, 31 October 2019.

8   Justin Scheck, Newley Purnell and Jeff Horwitz, 'Facebook employees flag drug cartels and human traffickers. The company's response is weak, documents show', *The Wall Street Journal*, 16 September 2021.

9   Will Feuer, 'YouTube's algorithm pushes violent content and misinformation: study', *New York Post*, 9 July 2021.

10 Sarah Manavis, 'Extreme radicalisation is happening on Facebook and YouTube – what can be done to stop it?', *New Statesman*, 15 December 2020 (updated 21 September 2021).

11 Jess Kung, 'What internet outrage reveals about race and TikTok's algorithm', *Code Switch*, NPR, 14 February 2022 and Alex Hern, 'TikTok "tried to filter out videos from ugly, poor or disabled users"', *The Guardian*, 18 March 2020.

12 Avani Dias, Jeanavive McGregor and Lauren Day, 'The TikTok spiral', *ABC News*, 26 July 2021.

Chapter 1: The Conspiracy Theorist

1   Patricia Cori, *The New Sirian Revelations: Galactic Prophecies for the Ascending Human Collective*, North Atlantic, 2017. The blurb appears online in several places; see, for example, www.amazon.com.au/ New-Sirian-Revelations-Prophecies-HumanCollective/dp/1623171717.

2   Mike Rothschild, *The Storm Is Upon Us: How QAnon Became a Movement, Cult and Conspiracy Theory of Everything*, Monoray, London, 2021.

3   David Weigel, 'The conspiracy theory behind a curious Roseanne Barr tweet, explained', *The Washington Post*, 31 March 2018.

4   Mike Rothschild, 'Jeff Sessions, the 2018 midterms, and the continued grift of QAnon', *Daily Dot*, 9 November 2018.

5   Mike McIntire, Karen Yourish and Larry Buchanan, 'In Trump's Twitter feed: conspiracy-mongers, racists and spies', *The New York Times*, 2 November 2019.

Notes

6   Gianluca Mezzofiore and Donie O'Sullivan, 'El Paso mass shooting is at
     least the third atrocity linked to 8chan this year', CNN, 5 August 2019.

7   Van Badham, *QAnon and On: A Short and Shocking History of Internet
     Conspiracy Cults*, Hardie Grant, Melbourne, 2021.

8   Rob Brotherton, *Suspicious Minds: Why We Believe Conspiracy Theories*,
     Bloomsbury, London, 2015.

9   Mick West, *Escaping the Rabbit Hole: How to Debunk Conspiracy Theories
     Using Facts, Logic, and Respect*, Skyhorse Publishing, New York, 2018.

10   Darlena Cunha, 'Red pills and dog whistles: it is more than "just the
     internet"', *Al Jazeera*, 6 September 2020.

11   Anthony Lantian, Dominique Muller, Cécile Nurra and Karen M. Douglas,
     '"I know things they don't know!: the role of need for uniqueness in belief in
     conspiracy theories', *Social Psychology*, vol. 48, no. 3, 10 July 2017; Edelson et
     al., 'The effect of conspiratorial thinking and motivated reasoning on belief
     in election fraud', *Political Research Quarterly*, vol. 70, no. 4, December 2017,
     pp. 933–46; Mike Wood, 'Propagating and debunking conspiracy theories
     on Twitter during the 2015–2016 Zika virus outbreak', *Cyberpsychology
     Behaviour and Social Networking*, vol. 21, no. 8, August 2018, pp. 485–90.

12   Andrew Marantz, 'Reddit and the struggle to detoxify the internet',
     The New Yorker, 12 March 2008.

13   Domingo Cullen, 'YouTube addiction: binge watching videos became my
     "drug of choice"', *The Guardian*, 3 May 2019 and Juan Flores, 'Ex-Facebook
     executive says company made its products as addictive as cigarettes', *CBS
     News*, 2 October 2020.

14   Chris O'Brien, 'NYU study: Facebook's content moderation efforts are
     "grossly inadequate"', *VentureBeat*, 7 June 2020.

15   Studies include: Cameron Ballard et al., 'Conspiracy brokers: understanding
     the monetization of YouTube conspiracy theories', New York University,
     31 May 2022; Kamille Grusauskaite et al., 'Picturing opaque power: how
     conspiracy theorists construct oppositional videos on YouTube', *Social Media
     + Society*, 22 April 2022; Nick Evershed et al., 'Anatomy of a conspiracy
     theory: how misinformation travels on Facebook', *The Guardian*, 11 March
     2021; and Axel Bruns et al., '"Corona? 5G? or both?": the dynamics of
     COVID-19/5G conspiracy theories on Facebook', *Media International
     Australia*, vol. 177, no. 1, 2020, pp. 12–29.

16   Steven Hassan, 'Influence Continuum', Freedom of Mind Centre, 2022.

17   While the 'backfire effect' is a popular theory among many, including
     psychologists, there is also research that questions its authenticity,

including work by academics Thomas Wood and Ethan Porter. Research by Cambridge University demonstrates that even highly partisan people can update their views on a topic when presented with accurate information. For further reading on this see, for example, Laura Hazard Owen, 'The "backfire effect" is mostly a myth, a broad look at the research suggests', *Nieman Journalism Lab*, 22 March 2019.

18 Steven Taylor, *The Psychology of Pandemics: Preparing for the Next Global Outbreak of Infectious Disease*, Cambridge Scholars Publishing, 2019, p. 65.

19 Mick West, 'How to debunk chemtrails', *Contrail Science: The Science and Pseudoscience of Contrails and Chemtrails*, 5 June 2011. Watch the video and view the photos at https://contrailscience.com/how-to-debunk-chemtrails/.

20 American Psychiatric Association, *Diagnostic and Statistical Manual of Mental Disorders*, 18 May 2013.

21 Mozilla, 'YouTube Regrets: a crowdsourced investigation into YouTube's recommendation algorithm', Mozilla Foundation, 7 July 2021; Abby Ohlheiser, 'How Covid-19 conspiracy theorists are exploiting YouTube culture', *MIT Technology Review*, 7 May 2020; and Brandy Zadrozny, 'Carol's journey: what Facebook knew about how it radicalized users', *NBC News*, 23 October 2021.

Chapter 2: The Freedom Fighter

1 Helen Lee Bouygues, 'Who's really driving the "freedom convoys"?' *Forbes*, 17 February 2022 and Shannon M. Smith, 'There's a history of white supremacists interpreting government leaders' words as encouragement', *The Conversation*, 18 May 2020.

2 No author, 'Covid: Huge protests across Europe over new restrictions', *BBC News*, 21 November 2021.

3 Rachel Pannett, 'Far-right activists blamed for fueling anti-vaccine mobs in Melbourne, Australia', *The Washington Post*, 21 September 2021.

4 Josh Butler, '"Occupy Canberra": behind the anti-vaccine protests at Parliament House', *The Guardian*, 4 February 2022.

5 Rachael Dexter and Simone Fox Koob, 'Falling into the "freedom" movement ... and getting out', *The Age*, 13 February 2022.

6 Michael McGowan, 'Where "freedom" meets the far right: the hate messages infiltrating Australian anti-lockdown protests', *The Guardian*, 26 March 2021.

7 AAP, 'Police say Melbourne anti-lockdown protest "most violent in nearly 20 years"', *The Guardian*, 22 August 2021.

8   Amelia McGuire, 'Convoy to Canberra protester arrested after police seize loaded rifle', *The Sydney Morning Herald*, 4 February 2022.

9   Christian Mack, 'Royal Commission & Senate Enquiry into the abuse of powers during Covid-19 (2020–2022)', Change.org, September 2022.

10   Thomas Aechtner, 'Distrust, danger, and confidence: a content analysis of the Australian Vaccination-Risks Network Blog', *Public Understanding of Science*, vol. 30, no. 1, January 2021 (first published 19 October 2020), pp. 16–35 and Rachael Dunlop, 'Anti-vaccination activists should not be given a say in the media', *The Guardian*, 16 October 2013. See also Zac Crellin, 'An anti-lockdowner raised $270k for legal fees even though her lawyers are working for free', *PedestrianTV*, 9 September 2021 and Tom Tanuki, 'How the anti-lockdown fundraising machine keeps running', *Independent Australia*, 11 September 2021.

11   Steven Taylor, *The Psychology of Pandemics: Preparing for the Next Global Outbreak of Infectious Disease,* Cambridge Scholars, Newcastle upon Tyne, 2019.

12   World Health Organization, 'Ten threats to global health in 2019', 2019.

13   Daniel Jolley and Karen M. Douglas, 'The effects of anti-vaccine conspiracy theories on vaccination intentions', *PLOS ONE*, vol. 9, no. 2, 20 February 2014.

14   Christina Steindl et al., 'Understanding psychological reactance: new developments and findings', *New Directions in Reactance Research*, vol. 223, no. 4, October 2015 (paraphrasing Jack and Sharon Brehm, *Psychological Reactance: A Theory of Freedom and Control*, Academic Press, New York, 1981).

15   Steven Taylor, *The Psychology of Pandemics*, pp. 89–90.

16   Sabina Kleitman et al., 'To comply or not comply? A latent profile analysis of behaviours and attitudes during the COVID-19 pandemic', *PLOS ONE*, vol. 16, no. 7, 29 July 2021 and No author, 'What psychology says about COVID non-compliers', The University of Sydney, 30 July 2021.

17   Lois Beckett, 'How Facebook and the White House let the "boogaloo" movement grow', *The Guardian*, 2 July 2020.

18   No author, 'Facebook's boogaloo problem: a record of failure', Tech Transparency Project, 12 August 2020.

19   Christopher Knaus and Michael McGowan, 'Who's behind Australia's anti-lockdown protests? The German conspiracy group driving marches', *The Guardian*, 27 July 2021.

20   Sarah McPhee and Jenny Noyes, 'TikTok star charged after anti-lockdown protest in hospital with COVID-19', *The Sydney Morning Herald*, 15 September 2021.

21   Denham Sadler, 'The role of social media in COVID protests', *Innovation Australia*, 27 July 2021.

22   'The Disinformation Dozen: why platforms must act on twelve leading online anti-vaxxers', Centre for Countering Digital Hate, 21 March 2021. Full report available at https://counterhate.com/research/the-disinformation-dozen/.

Chapter 3: The Social Media Narcissist

1   Oli Smith, 'Walrus drags zookeeper and tourist underwater and kills them in front of spectators', *Express*, 23 May 2016; Matt Siegel, 'Selfie madness: too many dying to get the picture', *Reuters*, 3 September 2015; and Mehmet Dokur et al., 'Media-based clinical research on selfie-related injuries and deaths', *Ulus Travma Acil Cerrahi Derg*, vol. 24, no. 2, March 2018, pp. 129–35.

2   Sopan Deb, 'Oops! A gallery selfie gone wrong causes $200,000 in damage', *The New York Times*, 14 July 2017.

3   Erving Goffman, *The Presentation of Self in Everyday Life*, Doubleday, Garden City, 1959, p. 86.

4   Riesman et al., *The Lonely Crowd: A Study of the Changing American Character* (revised edition), Yale University Press, New Haven, 2001.

5   Michael J. Rosenfeld and Reuben J. Thomas, 'Searching for a mate: the rise of the internet as a social intermediary', *American Sociological Review*, vol. 77, no. 4, 2012, pp. 523–47.

6   Sherry Turkle, *Alone Together: Why We Expect More from Technology and Less from Each Other*, Basic Books, New York, 2011, p. 183.

7   Trevor van Mierlo, 'The 1% rule in four digital health social networks: an observational study', *Journal of Medical Internet Research*, vol. 16, no. 2, February 2014, p. 32.

8   Dr C. George Boeree, 'A Bio-Social Theory of Neurosis', 2002, https://webspace.ship.edu/cgboer/genpsyneurosis.html.

9   No author, National Eating Disorders Association, 2022 and No author, Health Direct Australia, 2022.

10   No author, 'Key research and statistics', Eating Disorders Victoria, no date (figure in question dates from a 2012 study in *The Journal of Eating Disorders*) and No date, 'Why are eating disorders more common in the LGBTQ community?', Toledo Centre for Eating Disorders, 6 January 2022.

Notes

11 Jessica Baron, 'Does editing your selfies make you more likely to want plastic surgery?', *Forbes*, 27 June 2019; see also University of Texas Southwestern Medical Center, 'Selfies may drive plastic surgery by distorting facial features: cellphone images could alter the appearance of the nose and chin', *ScienceDaily*, 6 April 2022.

12 Hannah Paine, 'Melbourne "Barbie doll" woman reveals plans for another boob job', *News.com.au*, 27 August 2021 and Bianca Soldani, 'Model nearly dies trying to look like Barbie', *Yahoo Lifestyle*, 28 March 2018.

13 Jessica Bursztynsky and Lauren Feiner, 'Facebook documents show how toxic Instagram is for teens, *Wall Street Journal* reports', *CNBC Tech*, 14 September 2021, and Georgia Wells, Jeff Horwitz and Deepa Seetharaman, 'Facebook knows Instagram is toxic for teen girls, company documents show', *The Wall Street Journal*, 14 September 2021.

14 Emily A. Vogels, Risa Gelles-Watnick and Navid Massarat, 'Teens, social media and technology 2022', Pew Research Center, 10 August 2022.

15 Dale Carnegie, *How to Win Friends and Influence People in the Digital Age*, Simon & Schuster, New York, 2011, p. 159.

16 Sherry Turkle, *Alone Together*, pp. 271–72.

17 No author, 'More than 12M "Me Too" Facebook posts, comments, reactions in 24 hours', *CBS News*, 17 October 2017.

18 Karen Kaplan, 'After Alyssa Milano's #MeToo tweet, Google searches about sexual assault hit record high', *Los Angeles Times*, 21 December 2018.

19 Pranjal Mehar, '#MeToo increased awareness about sexual harassment: study', *Tech Explorist*, 23 December 2018.

20 Sally Engle Merry, 'Transnational human rights and local activism: mapping the middle', *American Anthropologist*, vol. 108, no. 1, 2006, pp. 38–51.

21 Jeffrey Lambert et al., 'Taking a one-week break from social media improves well-being, depression, and anxiety: a randomized controlled trial', *Cyberpsychology, Behavior and Social Networking*, vol. 25, no. 5, 10 May 2022.

22 Jordan Guiao, 'Insta-harms make Insta-money: how unregulated and unqualified social media influencers profit while spreading disinformation and causing harms online', *The Australia Institute's Centre for Responsible Technology Research Report*, September 2021.

23 'Code of Ethics', Australian Association of National Advertisers, 1 February 2021.

24   Melissa Coade, 'New TGA rules see influencers banned from health product promotions', *SmartCompany*, 7 March 2022.

Chapter 4: The Hateful Troll

1   Carly Findlay, 'How to win the internet. Or how to defend yourself when your photo is ridiculed on Reddit', *Carly Findlay*, 19 December 2013.

2   Ginger Gorman, *Troll Hunting*, Hardie Grant, Melbourne, 2019.

3   Ibid., p. 82.

4   No author, 'Supporting journalists to engage safely online', eSafety Commissioner, 2020.

5   Evita March, 'Psychopathy, sadism, empathy, and the motivation to cause harm: new evidence confirms malevolent nature of the internet troll', *Personality and Individual Differences*, vol. 141, 15 April 2019, pp. 133–37.

6   Evita March, 'New research shows trolls don't just enjoy hurting others, they also feel good about themselves', *The Conversation*, 16 September 2020.

7   Jim Macnamara, *Public Relations: Theories, Practices, Critiques*, Pearson Australia, Port Melbourne, 2012.

8   Jon Michail, 'Strong nonverbal skills matter now more than ever in this "new normal"', *Forbes*, 24 August 2020.

9   Heike Jacob et. al, 'Effects of emotional intelligence on the impression of irony created by the mismatch between verbal and nonverbal cues', *PLOS One*, 7 October 2016, and Markus Koppensteiner and Greg Siegle, 'Speaking through the body: do people associate the body movements of politicians with their speech?', *Politics and the Life Sciences*, vol. 36, no. 2, Fall 2017, pp. 104–13.

10   Tiffany O'Callaghan, 'Generosity can be contagious', *Time*, 8 March 2010.

11   M. J. Crockett, 'Moral outrage in the digital age', *Nature Human Behaviour*, vol. 1, no. 11, 2017, pp. 769–71.

12   Eli Pariser, 'Algorithmic catastrophe: how news feeds reprogram your mind and your habits', *Big Think*, 18 December 2018.

13   Roger McNamee, *Zucked: Waking Up to the Facebook Catastrophe*, Penguin Books, New York, 2019, p. 93.

14   Nicholas A. Christakis and James H. Fowler, *Connected: The Surprising Power of Our Social Networks and How They Shape Our Lives*, Little, Brown & Company, New York, 2009, p. 17.

15   Roger McNamee, *Zucked*, p. 242.

16 Ibid.

17 Dale Carnegie, *How to Win Friends and Influence People in the Digital Age*, p. 9.

18 Nicholas G. Carr, *The Shallows: What the Internet Is Doing to Our Brains*, W. W. Norton, New York, 2010, p. 131.

19 Nicholas Carr, 'Is the internet rotting our brains?', *Discover*, 26 March 2019.

20 No author, 'Google's Irene Au: on design challenges', *Bloomberg*, 19 March 2009.

21 Anagha Joshi and Trina Hinkley, 'Too much time on screens? Screen time effects and guidelines for children and young people', Child Family Community Australia project, Australian Institute of Family Studies, August 2021.

Chapter 5: The Dating App Pest

1 John Hendel, 'Old, weird tech: computer dating of the 1960s', *The Atlantic*, 15 February 2011.

2 John T. Cacioppo, 'Marital satisfaction and break-ups differ across on-line and off-line meeting venues', *Psychological and Cognitive Sciences*, 3 June 2013.

3 Mansoor Iqbal, 'Tinder Revenue and Usage Statistics (2022)', *Business of Apps*, 6 September 2022.

4 Aziz Ansari, 'Everything you thought you knew about love is wrong', *Time*, 28 June 2015.

5 Mansoor Iqbal, 'Tinder Revenue and Usage Statistics (2022)', *Business of Apps*, 6 September 2022.

6 Lucy Cavendish, 'Are you a midlife online dating addict?', *The Sydney Morning Herald*, 29 April 2018.

7 Ali Patillo, 'Dating app researchers offer advice for the socially anxious and awkward', *Inverse*, 3 August 2019.

8 Eli J. Finkel et al., 'Online dating: a critical analysis from the perspective of psychological science', *Psychological Science in the Public Interest*, vol. 13, no. 1, 2012, p. 49.

9 Nev Schulman, *In Real Life: Love, Lies & Identity in the Digital Age*, Hodder & Stoughton, London, 2014, p. 163.

10 Eli J. Finkel et al., 'Online dating: a critical analysis from the perspective of psychological science', p. 49.

11   Aziz Ansari and Eric Klinenberg, 'She'll text me, she'll text me not', *Nautilus Sociology*, 4 February 2016.

12   Joseph B. Walther and Monica T. Whitty, 'Language, psychology, and new new media: the hyperpersonal model of mediated communication at twenty-five years', *Journal of Language and Social Psychology*, vol. 40, no. 1, 2 November 2020, pp. 120–35.

13   Howard Gardner and Katie Davies, *The App Generation: How Today's Youth Navigate Identity, Intimacy, and Imagination in a Digital World*, Yale University Press, New Haven, 2013, p. 109.

14   Eli J. Finkel et al., 'Online dating: a critical analysis from the perspective of psychological science', p. 51.

15   Quoted in Mary Aitken, 'How is the internet changing the way we behave?', *BBC Science Focus*, 27 March 2017.

16   Aziz Ansari and Eric Klinenberg, *Modern Romance*, Penguin, New York, 2015, p. 121.

17   Howard Gardner and Katie Davies, *The App Generation* and Eli J. Finkel et al., 'Online dating: a critical analysis from the perspective of psychological science', p. 50.

18   Sheena S. Iyengar and Mark R. Lepper, 'When choice is demotivating: can one desire too much of a good thing?', *Journal of Personality and Social Psychology*, vol. 79, no. 6, 2000, pp. 995–1006.

19   No author, 'Safety by Design', eSafety Commissioner, no date.

Chapter 6: The Screen Addict

1   Sara Lebow, 'Gamers make up more than a third of the world's population', Insider Intelligence, *eMarketer*, 19 October 2021.

2   Jeffrey E. Brand et al., 'Digital Australia Report 2018', Interactive Games and Entertainment Association, 2018.

3   Jane McGonigal, *Reality Is Broken: Why Games Make Us Better and How They Can Change the World*, Penguin Books, New York, 2011, p. 2.

4   Elise Favis, 'How *The Sims* navigated 20 years of change to become one of the most successful franchises ever', *The Washington Post*, 4 February 2020.

5   Sherry Turkle, *Alone Together: Why We Expect More from Technology and Less from Each Other*, Basic Books, New York, 2011, p. 126.

6   Mary Aitken, *The Cyber Effect: A Pioneering Cyberpsychologist Explains How Human Behaviour Changes Online*, John Murray, London, 2016, p. 69.

7   Dr Vladimir Poznyak, 'Inclusion of "gaming disorder" in ICD-11', World Health Organization, 14 September 2018.

8   Mark Tran, 'Girl starved to death while parents raised virtual child in online game', *The Guardian*, 6 March 2010.

9   Jane Wakefield, '*Fortnite*: Is Prince Harry right to want game banned?', *BBC News*, 4 April 2019 and No author, '*Fortnite* is now even being blamed for divorce', *BBC News*, 17 September 2018.

10   Bill Browne, 'Gambling on games: how video games expose children to gambling', The Australia Institute Centre for Responsible Technology, February 2020.

11   Jari Katsyri et al., 'The opponent matters: elevated fMRI reward responses to winning against a human versus a computer opponent during interactive video game playing', *Cerebral Cortex*, vol. 23, no. 12, December 2013, pp. 2829–39.

12   Martin P. Paulus et al., 'Screen media activity and brain structure in youth: evidence for diverse structural correlation networks from the ABCD study', *NeuroImage*, vol. 185, January 2019, pp. 140–53.

13   Kevin Anderton, 'The impact of gaming: a benefit to society', *Forbes*, 25 June 2018.

14   Isabela Granic, Adam Lobel and Rutger C. M. E. Engels, 'The benefits of playing video games', *American Psychologist*, vol. 69, no. 1, January 2014, p. 73 and Jennifer Wilber, 'The many social benefits of playing video games', *Level Skip*, 25 November 2020.

15   Jennifer Wilber, 'The many social benefits of playing video games'.

16   Mihaly Csikszentmihalyi, *Flow: The Psychology of Optimal Experience*, Harper & Row, New York, 1990.

17   Edward Castranova, *Exodus to the Virtual World: How Online Fun Is Changing Reality*, St. Martin's Griffin, New York, 11 November 2008.

18   Jane McGonigal, *Reality Is Broken*, p. 64.

19   Clay Shirky, *Here Comes Everybody*, Penguin Books, New York, 2008.

20   Alex M. T. Russell et al., 'Social influences normalize gambling-related harm among higher risk gamblers', *Journal of Behavioral Addictions*, vol. 7, no. 4, December 2018, pp. 1100–11.

21   Mihaly Csikszentmihalyi, *Flow*.

Chapter 7: The Naive Futurist

1   Emily Dreyfuss, 'Facebook hires up three of its biggest privacy critics', *Wired*, 30 January 2019 and Johan Moreno, 'Google hires ex-Headspace executive amid ongoing digital health push', *Forbes*, 29 October 2021.

2   Alex Hern, 'As Mark Zuckerberg celebrates his 30th birthday, is Facebook maturing too?', *The Guardian*, 14 May 2014.

3   Peter Rubin, *Future Presence: How Virtual Reality is Changing Human Connection, Intimacy and the Limits of Ordinary Life*, Harper Collins, New York, 2018, p. 123.

4   Ibid., p. 120.

5   Helen Papagiannis, *Augmented Reality: How Technology Is Shaping the New Reality*, O'Reilly Media, Sebastopol, 2017, p. 20.

6   Leslie Jamison, 'The digital ruins of a forgotten future', *The Atlantic*, December 2017.

7   Ray Kurzweil, *The Singularity Is Near: When Humans Transcend Biology*, Penguin Books, New York, 2005.

8   Mark O'Connell, *To Be a Machine: Adventures Among Cyborgs, Utopians, Hackers, and the Futurists Solving the Modest Problem of Death*, Granta, London, 2017, p. 2.

9   Ibid., pages unknown.

10 Ray Kurzweil, *The Singularity Is Near: When Humans Transcend Biology*, Penguin Books, New York, 2005.

11 Emile P. Torres, 'Elon Musk, Twitter and the future: his long-term vision is even weirder than you think', *Salon*, 30 April 2022

12 No author, 'Antitrust: Commission fines Google €2.42 billion for abusing dominance as search engine by giving illegal advantage to own comparison shopping service', European Commission, 27 June 2017.

13 This quote is commonly attributed to actor André De Shields but it has also been attributed to others, such as spiritualist Marianne Williamson.

Conclusion

1   The White House, 'A Declaration for the Future of the Internet', 28 April 2022.

Lightning Source UK Ltd.
Milton Keynes UK
UKHW041132041122
411641UK00004B/560